COLUMBIA PAPYRI XI

AMERICAN STUDIES IN PAPYROLOGY

Series Editor
Ann Ellis Hanson

Number 38

COLUMBIA PAPYRI XI

Timothy M. Teeter

COLUMBIA PAPYRI XI

TIMOTHY M. TEETER

SCHOLARS PRESS
ATLANTA, GEORGIA

COLUMBIA PAPYRI XI

TIMOTHY M. TEETER

The publication of this book was assisted by a grant from the
Stanwood Cockey Lodge Foundation
of Columbia University

Library of Congress Cataloging in Publication Data

Teeter, Timothy M.
Columbia papyri XI / Timothy M. Teeter.
p. cm. — (American studies in papyrology ; no. 38)
Revisions of the author's thesis (Ph.D.) — Columbia University, 1989, under the title: Ten Christian papyri in the Columbia collection.
Includes bibliographical references and index.
ISBN 0-7885-0433-9 (alk. paper)
1. Manuscripts, Greek (Papyri) 2. Columbia University. Rare Book and Manuscript Library. 3. Manuscripts, Greek—New York (State)—New York. 4. Christian literature, Early—Manuscripts. I. Title. II. Series: American studies in papyrology ; v. 38.
PA3305.C645 1998
091'.0938—dc21 97-47717
CIP

Printed in the United States of America
on acid-free paper

CONTENTS

Preface

The present volume has its origins in my dissertation, *Ten Christian Papyri in the Columbia Collection,* for which I received my doctorate from Columbia University in 1989. I had taken a course in papyrology with Roger Bagnall while a graduate student, and it was he who suggested the idea of editing a group of previously unpublished papyri, all with some connection with the early Christian church. Roger's guidance and encouragement have been instrumental first in completing the dissertation and then in revising it for publication.

Along with Roger, many others have read all or part of this work at various stages, and their help has been considerable. I first edited what is now **293** in this volume, a New Testament fragment, as part of Roger's course, and the result was read and commented on by Bruce Metzger. Klaas Worp assisted with several difficult readings while I was completing the dissertation. My dissertation defense committee—Alan Cameron, William Harris, the late John Meyendorff, and especially the late Morton Smith—all read the dissertation, and their comments and corrections considerably improved it. The finished dissertation was read by Dieter Hagedorn, G.H.R. Horsley, and the late Kurt Treu, all of whom contributed many corrections and suggestions. John Oates deserves thanks for making the papyrus room at Duke University so readily available. Ann Ellis Hanson and the anonymous referees for the American Society of Papyrologists who read the manuscript made many corrections and encouraged further work and reflection on several points. Thanks are also due to the staff of the Rare Books and Manuscripts room of Butler Library at Columbia University. The individual who undoubtedly showed the most patience, however, is my wife Toni, to whom this work is dedicated with affection and appreciation.

A Faculty Research Grant from Georgia Southern University enabled me to spend the summer of 1992 at Columbia revising the dissertation.

My dissertation has been listed in the *Checklist of Editions of Greek Papyri and Ostraca* as *P.Col.Teeter.* The present work is not a reprint but a substantial revision, with an additional papyrus that did not appear in the dissertation. A concordance is given at the end.

Table of Papyri

Literary/Liturgical Texts

Documentary Texts

List of Plates

Editorial Conventions

All texts in this volume are edited according to the standard "Leiden" system fixed in 1931 and described by Eric G. Turner in *Greek Papyri: An Introduction* (New York 1980) 187-8, 203.

α̣β̣γ̣δ̣	Letters either uncertain themselves or if they were read out of context.
αβγδ] or [αβγδ] or [αβγδ	Lost letters restored by conjecture
⟨αβγδ⟩	Letters or words omitted by the scribe and supplied by the editor.
(αβγδ)	Abbreviations resolved by the editor
[[αβγδ]]	Letters or words written, then canceled, by the scribe.
\`αβγδ´	Letters or words added by the scribe above the line.
. . . . .	Unreadable traces of letters, of which the number is estimated.
[. .] or [± 2]	Lacuna, due to a hole, fading, abrasion or tear, in which the number of lost letters is estimated.
] or [ ] or [	Lacuna in which the number of letters lost is unknown.
⟨ ⟩	Letters or words wrongly omitted by the scribe, if they cannot be supplied.

The critical apparatus supplies all corrections for departures from standard, classical Greek. Punctuation, accents and breathings are added; in the case of incorrect forms, accents are added as if they were spelled correctly, unless the word is indecipherable. Case errors are corrected in the apparatus and not supplied in angle brackets. Diaeresis in the text is noted in the apparatus. In giving the dimensions of the papyri, the breadth of the recto comes first, followed by the height.

Papyrus editions and papyrological journals are cited according to *Checklist of editions of Greek and Latin papyri, ostraca and tablets* ed. J.F. Oates, R.S. Bagnall, W.H. Willis, K.A. Worp, 4th ed. (*BASP* Suppl. no. 7 1992). Other journals are cited according to the practice of *TAPA* or

L'Année Philologique. Books and reference works cited by short title or abbreviation are listed in the bibliography. Other works are cited in full when they first appear and subsequently by the author's name. Patristic references are to the editions listed in *Thesaurus Linguae Graecae Canon of Greek authors and works*, ed. Luci Berkowitz and Karl A. Squitier, 3rd ed. (New York 1990) unless otherwise noted. I have given the reference to Migne's *Patrologia* when that is the edition used by the *TLG*.

TEXTS

Literary/Liturgical Texts

293. Matt. 6:4-6, 8-12

Inv. 571 | 7.1 x 6.2 cm. | V
Pl. 1 | | Provenance unknown

This fragment of the Gospel according to Matthew, containing most of the Lord's Prayer and four verses of the introduction, is written on a badly damaged parchment codex leaf. The damage may be due to water, or exposure to extreme heat, or both; whatever the case, it is badly wrinkled, smudged, worn through in spots and very faded. Many letters are lost in whole or in part, while others may be seen only by patient examination under magnification. Text is missing both at top and bottom, and the left edge of the recto is ragged, possibly from the page's having been torn out. The circumstances of its separation from the codex are mysterious; if it was torn out to be kept as a charm or used for recitation, whoever did so was careless and lost the last portion of the prayer.[1]

The right edge of the recto is clearly the right edge of the original page. Approximately fourteen lines are missing between the end of the recto and the beginning of the verso, making the total number of lines in the column 27 or 28. Using the better preserved text at the right edge of the recto as a measure, the height of ten lines is 4.5 cm., making the height of the column approximately 12 to 13 cm. Adding top and bottom margins, the piece would originally have been perhaps 16 or 17 cm. high.

---

1 There is no Greek text of the Lord's Prayer on papyrus that was not created to be an amulet or toy; K. Aland, ed., *Repertorium der Griechischen Christlichen Papyri, I: Biblische Papyri* (Berlin and New York 1976) 351-5, 397; van Haelst, *Catalogue* 128-130. The original editor of *P.Ant.* II 54 suggested that it may have been a "toy book for a child." The suggestion is repeated by Aland.

The width at its broadest is 7.1 cm, of which 2.3 is margin and 4.8 is text. Since the text is missing only one letter at the piece's broadest point, and since the average letter is .2 cm. wide, the column would have been 5 cm. broad. If the codex were only a single column per page, then, allowing for an additional margin on the left, the total width would have been approximately 9.6 cm. However, if there had been a (now missing) column to the left on the recto (and right on the verso), an additional column plus some space in between the two columns would make the page approximately 16 to 17 cm. wide.

We are left with two choices: 1) a page 9.6 cm. wide by 16 to 17 cm. high or 2) 16-17 cm. wide by 16-17 cm. high. Eric Turner gives a list of 165 parchment codices, classified by dimensions. Choice 1) would barely qualify as a miniature "pocket" Bible (defined as breadth < 10 cm. and height < twice breadth), but would still be larger than any of the 45 miniatures Turner lists. Although the top and bottom margins could be larger than estimated here, Turner lists only two parchment codices out of 165 where breadth < 10 cm. and height = approximately twice breadth. On the other hand, the "square" type, with the breadth only just shorter than the height, is common, which favors choice 2). Several on Turner's list have dimensions close to 2), though only two have a breadth of 16 cm.[2]

The hand is a fine "biblical" hand, similar to those of the Codex Alexandrinus[3] and *P.Oxy.* VI 848, plate I, favoring a fifth century date. The down strokes are firm, although not thick, while the horizontal strokes are so fine that they are gone due to fading; the horizontal bar of every pi has completely vanished. Although there are no lectionary signs, the scribe has separated sections by leaving blank spaces, either at the end of a line or, in line 11 of the recto, approximately .6 cm between the first and second words. Why there is also a space (if that is what it is, and not simply fading) before the αὐτόν of the verso, line 2, is a mystery.

The text agrees in all major respects with the 27th edition of N(estle)-A(land), as well as the Codex Sinaiticus (א) and the Codex

2 E. G. Turner, *The Typology of the Early Codex* (Philadelphia 1977) 26-32. On miniatures, see also W.H. Worrell, *The Coptic Manuscripts in the Freer Collection*, (Univ. of Michigan studies. Humanistic series, vol. 10 1923) xi-xiii; A. Henrichs, L. Koenen, "Ein griechischer Mani-Codex," *ZPE* 5 (1970) 100-3.

3 See *Facsimile of the Codex Alexandrinus*, vol. 4: *The New Testament and Clementine Epistles* (London 1879) and *The Codex Sinaiticus and the Codex Alexandrinus with Seven Illustrations* (London 1955). Several hands of course produced the Codex Alexandrinus; see H. J. M. Milne and T. C. Skeat, *Scribes and Correctors of the Codex Sinaiticus* (1938) 91-3.

Vaticanus (B). Alternate readings from several important uncials are given below to show the type of text, which appears to be Alexandrian.[4]

Recto: [σου ὁ βλέπων ἐν τ]ῷ κ[ρυπτῷ] *6.4*
[ἀπ]οδώσει σοι.
[κα]ὶ [ὅταν] π̣ροσεύχησθε, *6.5*
[ο]ὐκ [ἔσε]σθ̣[ε] ὡς οἱ ὑποκρι-
[ταί·] ὅ̣τ̣ι̣ φιλοῦσιν ἐν ταῖς
[σ]υνα̣γ̣ωγα̣ῖ̣ς̣ [κ]αὶ ἐν ταῖς
[γων]ί̣α̣ι̣ς̣ τῶν [πλατ]ειῶν
[ἑσ]τῶτες προσεύχεσθαι,
[ὅ]πως φανῶσι τοῖς ἀν(θρώπ)οις·
[ἀ]μὴν [λέ]γω ὑμῖν, ἀπέ-
χ̣ουσι τὸν μισθὸν αὐ-
[τ]ῶν. *vacat* σὺ δὲ ὅταν προσ- *6.6*
[ε]ύχῃ, εἴσελθε̣ ε̣ἰς τὸ τα-
[μιεῖόν σου καὶ κλείσ]α̣ς̣

Verso: *vacat* αὐτόν. *vacat* *6.8*
οὕ[τ]ως οὖν προσεύχ[εσθε] *6.9*
ὑμεῖς· Πάτερ ἡμῶν ὁ [ἐν]
τοῖς οὐρανοῖ[ς], ἁγι̣[ασθή-]
τω [τὸ ὄνομά σο]υ, ἐ̣λθ̣[ά-] *6.10*
τω ἡ̣ [βασιλ]εία σου, [γ]ε̣ν̣[η-]
θ̣[ή]τω τὸ θέλημά σου, ὡ̣[ς]
[ἐν ο]ὐ̣ρανῷ κ̣α̣ὶ ἐπὶ γῆς.

---

4 A summary of the major MSS according to type may be found in B. Metzger, *A Textual Commentary on the Greek New Testament* (United Bible Societies 1971) xxviii-xxxi. For a full apparatus of variant readings in Matthew, see S.C.E. Legg, *Novum Testamentum Graece secundum textum Westcotto-Hortianum: Evangelium Secundum Matthaeum* (Oxford 1940).

τὸ̣[ν] ἄ̣ρτον ἡμῶν τὸν [ἐ-] *6.11*
πιούσιον δὸς ἡμῖν σή̣-
μερον· καὶ ἄφες ἡμῖν [τὰ] *6.12*
12 ὀφειλή̣μ̣α̣τα ἡμῶν, ὡ[ς]
κ̣α̣ὶ̣ [

Recto: 9 ἀνοις

Recto: 2 σοι N-A, ℵ B Z; σοι ἐν τῷ φανερῷ E K L M S U W D Y P

3-4 προσεύχησθε οὐκ ἔσεσθε N-A, ℵ B Z; προσεύχῃ οὐκ ἔσῃ D E K L M S U D Y P

4 ὡς N-A, ℵ B D Z; ὥσπερ E K L M S U D P

5 ταῖς The final sigma is very small, written at the top of, but not above, the line, something not uncommon in uncial MSS. It may also be the work of the corrector suggested for line 9.

9 ὅπως N-A, ℵ B D K L Z; ὅπως ἄν E M S U D Y

φανῶσι = φανῶσιν N-A

ανοις = ἀνθρώποις The -οις is written in the same fashion as the final sigmas of line 6, and at first sight would appear to be the standard form of a *nomen sacrum*. That is how I have treated it in resolving the abbreviation in the text. However, the customary line drawn over a *nomen sacrum* is missing (though this may be due to fading). A mixture of abbreviated and non-abbreviated forms of the *nomina sacra* is not uncommon; see Paap, *Nomina Sacra* and José O'Callaghan, *Nomina Sacra in Papyris Graecis Saeculi III Neotestamentariis* (Rome 1970). Still, it seems odd that the scribe would abbreviate a profane use of ἄνθρωπος while neglecting to abbreviate a sacred πάτηρ and οὐρανός. Πάτερ and οὐρανοῖς are abbreviated in the same passage of ℵ, while ἀνθρώποις is not. In B πάτερ and οὐρανοῖς are not abbreviated, but neither is ἀνθρώποις. Just possibly, the scribe simply forgot to write θρωποις at the beginning of the next line, and either he or a later corrector, unable or unwilling to extend the word into the margin, wrote only the final syllable. The ink of -οις is noticeably darker than the rest of the line.

10-11 ἀπέχουσι ℵ; ἀπέχουσιν N-A, B D Z; ὅτι ἀπέχουσιν E K L M S U D Y P

Verso: 3 It is very difficult to be certain, but there may be a colon just after the ὑμεῖς, followed by a short space.

8 ἐπὶ γῆς N-A, א B Z; ἐπὶ τῆς γῆς D E G K L M S U Y P *P.Ant.* II 54

294. Prayer and Ps. 150 3b-6

Inv. 97 6.5 x 10 cm. IV
Pl. 2 Provenance unknown

The papyrus is dark and dirty, severely faded or worn in spots, with a hole in line 2 and in the center of the space between lines 8 and 9 of the verso. However, the ink is dark and much the greater part of the text is clearly visible, if not easily legible. The hand, evidently the same on both recto and verso, is a graceless semi-cursive; on the recto the letters are often crowded and smudged. The hand is not consistent, perhaps from impatience—after five lines of the recto, the epsilon of ἐν changes into an s-curve.

The text of the recto, apparently a fragment of Psalm 150, begins in the middle of the psalm. The initial letters of lines 4 and 6 are higher than the remainder of their respective lines, and appear to be, together with lines 9 and 10, the ends of lines that originated in a lost column to the left. The scribe evidently started to write at the top of the remaining portion of the papyrus further to the left than neatness would require and shifted the column right when the (now mostly missing) left column intruded. The text of the verso appears to begin with the first line; there is no indication of any other text either to the left or above. A vertical crease approximately 2 to 2.5 centimeters from the left edge of the verso suggests the papyrus was folded there. A similar fold on the right side of the original document would account for the clean break on the right edge. Since the document was apparently saved for the sake of the text on the verso, such folds imply its use as an amulet. The folds, the direction of the fibres and the relative state of preservation of the texts on each side indicate that the verso was written separately and after the recto.

The prayer on the verso can be called a litany, but it is not a typical one. The use of ἐλέησον or Κύριε ἐλέησον or some other variation can be traced back through the life of the early church, the New Testament, the Septuagint (Ps. 6:3, 40:5, 11, etc.), to pagan practice. However, the earliest references to Κύριε ἐλέησον as a formal refrain are fourth century descriptions of a series of petitions with Κύριε ἐλέησον as a response.[5] This document is not a series of requests, nor is it addressed to a multitude of divine powers (Cf. *P.Oxy.* VIII 1152). It is a list of divine titles or epithets, of which the first seven at least, and perhaps all, are preceded or followed by ἐλέησον, something not precisely paralleled by anything we know of from the period.

Similar language or groups of titles such as these are found in several places, however, in early liturgical literature:

> Σὺ γὰρ δέσποτα ἐπουράνιε βασιλεῦ τῶν αἰώνων . . . (1 Clem. 61.2)
>
> [Σε] ἐπικαλοῦμαι δέσποτα παντοκρά-/[τ]ορ ἐπουράνιε ἐπίσκοπε πανάρε-/[τ]ε Θεὲ . . .[6]
>
> σὺ δέσποτα παντοκράτορ Θεὲ αἰώνιε . . .[7]
>
> δέσποτα κύριε παντοκράτωρ ἐπουράνιε . . .[8]

Although the fragment is small, there are several clues to the character of the scribe and document. He knew how to write; that is, he was more than a βραδέως γράφων, someone who has memorized how to write his name and a select phrase or two without actually being literate.[9] He understood the principle of the *nomen sacrum.* He also knew some biblical phrases and the kind of language likely to be heard in a liturgy.

On the other hand, he was uncertain of his spelling; his use of the *nomen sacrum* was atypical; his hand was unpractised and sloppy. Moreover, his use of language suggests that he did not fully understand the meaning of all the words he wrote. 'Αμίαντος is rare as a description

---

5 J.A. Jungmann, *The Mass of the Roman Rite: Its Origins and Development,* trans. F.A. Brunner (New York 1951-1955) 333-345.

6 Deir el-Bala'izah papyrus, fol.1 v lines 10-12, from "Der liturgische Papyrus von Deir el - Bala'izah in Oberägypten," ed. K. Gamber, *Muséon* 82 (1969) 66.

7 *Apostolic Constitutions* VIII.25.3 in *Didascalia et Constitutiones Apostolorum,* ed. F .X. Funk (Paderborn 1905).

8 The Liturgy of St. Mark in *Liturgies Eastern and Western,* vol. 1, *Eastern Liturgies,* ed. F. E. Brightman (Oxford 1896) 133.

9 H. C. Youtie, "Βραδέως γράφων: Between literacy and illiteracy," and "AGRAMMATOS: An aspect of Greek society in Egypt," *Scriptiunculae* (Amsterdam 1973-76) II 611-651.

of God. Δεωμεθε (= δεόμεθα) comes in the middle of a list of divine *titles*, and the scribe ends it with an epsilon as though it were a vocative like the others above it; could he have thought it was a noun? He follows δέσποτα with οὐράνια, not οὐράνιε, which suggests that he only changed the ending of a noun when he was phonetically certain, as he would likely be with δέσποτα, then made whatever came after follow suit.

The different titles and terms of the verso are perhaps not a random selection of words and phrases strung together from Scripture and the liturgies, but may be tied together by a common thread. In particular, lines 3-5 and 11-13 (addressing Abraham, Isaac and Jacob) may indicate a *funerary* theme.

The *Didascalia Apostolorum* of the third century instructs believers to "come together even in the cemeteries, and read the Holy Scriptures" together with celebrating the Eucharist at funerals and on the anniversaries of the deaths of the faithful.[10] In a description of burial rites c. 500 by Ps.-Dionysius we find, "The λειτουργοί then read the text of the faithful promises contained in the divine Scriptures on the subject of our resurrection and sing psalms relating to the same theme" (PG3.556C).[11] What two texts would be more likely to be read here than 1 Peter 1:3-4, "By his great mercy we have been born anew to a living hope through the resurrection of Jesus Christ from the dead, and to an inheritance which is imperishable, undefiled, and unfading (εἰς κληρονομίαν ἄφθαρτον καὶ ἀμίαντον καὶ ἀμάραντον), kept in heaven for you," and Matthew 22:31-32, "And as for the resurrection of the dead, have you not read what was said to you by God, Ἐγώ εἰμι ὁ Θεὸς Αβρααμ καὶ ὁ Θεὸς Ισαακ καὶ ὁ Θεὸς Ιακωβ; He is not the God of the dead but of the living"?

The latter phrase especially is found, in one form or another, over and over again in early prayers for the dead, e.g., *Didascalia Apostolorum* VI.22,[12] the *Apostolic Constitutions* VIII.41, and in a prayer for the dead from the fourth century euchologion of Bishop Serapion of Thmuis:

> Ὁ Θεὸς ὁ ζωῆς καὶ θανάτου τὴν ἐξουσίαν ἔχων, ὁ Θεὸς ὁ τῶν πνευμάτων καὶ δεσπότης πάσης σαρκός . . . μόνος αὐτὸς ἄφθαρτος καὶ ἀναλλοίωτος καὶ αἰώνιος

---

[10] *Didascalia Apostolorum: The Syriac Version Translated and Accompanied by the Verona Latin Fragments*, trans. and ed. R. H. Connolly (Oxford 1929) 252.

[11] See D. Rutledge, *Cosmic Theology: The Ecclesiastical Hierarchy of Pseudo-Denys* (London 1964) 189.

[12] Chapter 26 in Connolly 252.

ὤν· δεόμεθά σου περὶ τῆς κοιμήσεως καὶ ἀναπαύσεως τοῦ δούλου σου . . . ἐν ταμείοις ἀναπαύσεως μετὰ Ἀβραὰμ καὶ Ισαὰκ καὶ Ιακὼβ καὶ πάντων τῶν ἁγίων σου . . . (underlining mine).[13]

This liturgical phraseology appears in funerary inscriptions as well. In one such epitaph from 409 AD, God is requested to ensure that the loved one dwells εἰς κόλπους τῶν ἁγίων πατέρων/ Ἀβρααμ Ἰσακ καὶ Ἰακωβ, a liturgical conflation of Luke 16:22 and Matthew 22:31-32.[14] The same phrase appears in a sixth century letter of condolence, *P.Oxy.* XVI 1874. An inscription from 'Abu Sha'ar dated by the editors to the 5th-6th century begins δέομαι σου κ(ύρι)ε ὦ θ(εὸ)ς τῶν πα/τέρων ἡμῶν Ἀβραὰμ καὶ Ἰσα/ὰκ καὶ Ἰακὼβ.[15]

Almost all the material, both recto and verso, consists of memorable phrases easily taken from a common biblical-liturgical stock. Even rarities such as ἀμίαντος are not so odd when viewed this way. There is an alliterative-repetitive quality on both sides. Psalm 150 could not have been copied, given the mispellings; it must have been produced from memory.

All of this suggests a Christian of minimal literacy in Greek, impressed by matters relating to burial and the question of immortality, who composed a "private" litany which he subse-quently kept as an amulet. A religious interest in matters concerning the dead is hardly unusual in Egypt, and the use of liturgical formulas surrounding the dead as an amulet is not unknown, e.g., *P.Ryl.* III 465.[16]

---

[13] Chapter 50 in Funk 194.

[14] No. 48 in *Recueil des inscriptions grecques-chrétiennes d'Égypte,* ed. Gustave Lefebvre (Cairo 1907). This text is republished with commentary by G. H. R. Horsley in *New Docs 1978* 105-109, no. 89, where he lists several other epitaphs with the same or similar formula.

[15] R. S. Bagnall and J. Sheridan, "Documents from 'Abu Sha'ar, 1992-1993," *BASP* 31 (1994) 114-5. The text given here is the normalized version of the editors. See also A. Latjar, "Varia Nubica III: Ein liturgisches Gebet aus Qasr Ibrim," *ZPE* 112 (1996) 140-2 for other instances of citing the patriarchs in liturgical papyri and inscriptions.

[16] The degree to which Christianity served as an inspiration for acquiring literacy is disputed. It has been asserted that Christianity encouraged literacy; see A. von Harnack, *Über den privaten Gebrauch der Heiligen Schriften in der alten Kirche* (Leipzig 1912); also Ewa Wipszycka, "Le degré d'alphabétisation en Égypte Byzantine," *REAug* 30 (1984) 288: "D'ailleurs, le rôle stimulant de l'évangélisation n'était pas restreint à la mise en place d'un vaste appareil ecclésiastique, mais s'étendait à la propagation de la lecture de l'Écriture et des textes de dévotion, dont la connaissance était inséparable de la foi. Pour des hommes extrêmement sensibles

The suggestion of a near-literate devotional exercise based on familiar liturgical phrases is strengthened by the only papyrus I know of that in any way parallels **294**, published by Kurt Treu and dated by him to the fourth or fifth century.[17] The hand is a large semi-cursive like ours, but considerably neater, and the writer also has trouble spelling, though not so much as **294**. The recto has 23 lines of a somewhat disjointed and repetitive prayer (or prayers). There are several puzzles in the text, the greatest being the expression λευλευ.[18] λευλευ also appears on the verso of Treu's text, which oddly recalls the verso of **294**:

aux choses de la religion, et ils étaient légion en Égypte, c'était là un motif suffiçant pour essayer d'apprendre au moins à lire." However, W. V. Harris, *Ancient Literacy* (Harvard 1989) 316-22, esp. 321, concludes that Christianity's disaffection from classical pagan culture may have contributed somewhat to a decline in literacy in late anitquity.

On the other hand, organized monasticism enouraged literacy among its adherents, Wipszycka 291-295, though her conclusions are far too optimistic for Harris 303-4. As well, and despite the odd case of an illiterate lector (*P.Oxy.* XXXIII 2673), the great majority of the clergy were literate and were expected to be so; some of the ancient canons required the clergy to be literate. See Wipszycka, "Le degré d'alphabétisation en Égypte Byzantine," *REAug* 30 (1984) 288-89, Harris 320-21, and R. S. Bagnall, *Egypt* 248-49. On the illiterate lector see G. W. Clarke, *ZPE* 57 (1984) 103-4, but also the objections of E. Wipszycka, "Les ordres mineurs dans l'Église d'Égypte du IIe au VIIIe siècle," *JJurPap* 23 (1993) 212-215.

17 No. 4 in K. Treu, "Varia Christiana II," *APF* 32 (1986) 25-34.

18 On the λευλευ formula, see *P.Berl. Sarischouli* 2, note to line 2, where the expression also occurs. *P.Berl. Sarischouli* 2 is another text with repetitive liturgical formulae and a series of divine predicates. Among the possibilities suggested by Treu and Sarischouli for the source of λευλευ are magic, an abbreviation of Βασιλεῦ, Βασιλεῦ, or an abbreviation of αλληλουια. Both believe that the λευλευ ελεησον on the verso of P.Berol. inv. 21251 eliminates the possibility that λευλευ could itself be a form of ελεησον. However, this presumes a consistency and clarity on the part of the scribe that the text itself does not encourage. The similarities between *P.Col.* **294** and P.Berl. inv. 21251 suggest that some form of ελεησον should not be ruled out.

P.Berol. inv. 21251 verso

\+

εις θεο[ς ελε]ησον ει⟨ς⟩ θεος ελεη̣⟨σον⟩ . .

λευλευ ελεησον
λευλευ κυριε
λ̣ευλευ δεομεθα
λευλευ επακουσαν
λευλευ αορατε
λευ[λ]ευ αμιαντε
λευ[λευ δ]ικαιε
λευ[λευ κυρ]ιε
]υ̣ε

Both P.Berol. inv. 21251 and **294** use some of the same terms. Both are on the verso of repetitive, formulaic Christian texts, and are themselves even more repetitive and formulaic. Both have a mix of biblical and non-biblical vocabulary, as well as biblical words used in a non-biblical sense (αμιαται, *sc.* ἀμίαντε) and verbs possibly treated as nouns (δεωμεθε, δεόμεθα). Both appear to be biblical-liturgical composites. Despite all this, no direct connection between the two texts can be demonstrated. Rather, the two texts are products of a similar set of needs and circumstances: piety, exposure to liturgy, and perhaps a desire for literacy.

Recto: αἰνεῖτα̣ι [α]ὐτὸν ἐν ψ̣[αλτηρίῳ καὶ κιθάρᾳ
α̣ἰνεῖται αὐτὸν ἐν [τυμπάνῳ καὶ χορῷ
αἰνεῖται αὐτὸν ἐν χ̣[ορδαῖς καὶ ὀργάνῳ
\` ν̣ ´ αἰνεῖται αὐτὸν ἐ̣ν̣[κυμβάλοις εὐήχοις
αἰνεῖται αὐτόν ἐ̣ν̣[κυμβάλοις ἀλαλαγμοῦ
\` . ´ πᾶσα π̣[νοὴ] α̣ἰ̣ν̣ε̣[σάτω τὸν κύριον
. . . . [
α̣ὐ̣τῶν
] . . . αὐτῶν̣

Verso: ✱μ
ἐλέυσω[ν] κ̅υ̅
ἅγιε ἐλέησων
4 ἀμίαται ἐλέησων
ἄφθαρτ ` ε ΄ λέησων
δεώμεθε ἐλέησω̣[ν]
δέσπο̣τα ἐλέησω[ν]
8 οὐράν̣ι̣α̣ ἐλέησ̣ω̣[ν]
ὦ χω̣ορ̣γυσων πιν[
ὦ Θεὼς τῶν ἐών̣[ων]
ὦ Θεὼς ῎Αρ̅μ̅ο̅ς̅
12 ὦ Θεὸς Ἰσάκ̣
[ὦ] Θ̣εὸς Ἰ̣ακ̣[ώβ]

Recto: αἰνεῖται = αἰνεῖτε
Verso: 2-8 ἐλέυσων, ἐλέησων = ἐλέησον
2 κ̅υ̅ = κυρίου or κύριε 4 ἀμίαται = ἀμίαντε
6 δεώμεθε = δεόμεθα 8 οὐράνια = οὐράνιε
9 χωοργυσων πιν[= χορηγήσων πεινῶσιν? 9-10 Θεὼς = Θεὸς
10 ἐώνων = αἰώνων 11 ῎Αρ̅μ̅ο̅ς̅ = ῎Αβραμος

(Verso) . . . Have mercy, Lord. Holy one, have mercy. Undefiled one, have mercy. Incorruptible one, have mercy. We beseech (?), have mercy. Master, have mercy. Heavenly one, have mercy. O supplier to the hungry (?) . . . O God of the ages . . . O God of Abraham . . . O God of Isaac . . . O God of Jacob . . .

Recto: I have supplied the text for several lines where the papyrus breaks off. However, given the fragmentary state of the papyrus, it is impossible to know how well the scribe remembered Psalm 150. The psi and chi at the end of αἰνεῖται αὐτὸν ἐν in lines 1 and 3 can only be supplied on the basis of the known text of Psalm 150. Verse six of Psalm

150 appears to start at the beginning of line 7, but after the initial letters the ink becomes so faded and the papyrus so torn that nothing else can be made out with any certainty.

Verso: 1 The most reasonable interpretation of the two letters of line 1 would be XMΓ, with the final gamma omitted. This is not surprising if, as we have suggested, the author had only a hazy idea of what he was writing. The first letter, however, looks like a chi with an extra horizontal stroke through the middle, like a large asterisk. On the meaning of XMΓ, see most recently the remarks by Tomasz Derda in *Deir el-Naqlun: The Greek Papyri* (*P.Naqlun* I) (Warsaw 1995) 179-187. Derda cites several instances where the final gamma of XMΓ is omitted.

3-5 should probably be linked together. Ἀμίαντος, "undefiled," "pure," is a common classical word used in philosophy, religion, and magic (*Pap.Graec.Mag.* 289), but rarely as a description of, or name for, God. A check of eighty-one Christian and related authors and works in the TLG Data Bank Texts of the *Thesaurus Linguae Graecae Pilot CD ROM #D* shows its use to be uncommon as an epithet for ὁ Θεός, though it is used occasionally for Christ and frequently for the Virgin. Its use in the Septuagint is very rare, and it is not an adjective for God. It is an attribute of Christ once in the New Testament (Hebrews 7:26). PGL gives only three references of its use as an epithet for God in the patristic period: twice in Methodius Olympius, *Symposium* 1.1 (PG.18.37a) and 2.2 (PG18.49b), and once in the *Martyrium Theodoti*. It occurs once in a list of divine epithets for ὁ θεός, not unlike those in **294**, in the *Acts of John* 107: ὁ ἀγαθὸς ἡμῶν θεός, ὁ εὔσπλανγχνος, ὁ ἐλεήμων, ὁ ἅγιος, ὁ καθαρός, ὁ ἀμίαντος, *κτλ.* Ἄφθαρτος is more widely used in magic, the New Testament (e.g., 1 Tim. 1:17), and the theological and liturgical literature. The two are found together, however, in an alliterative phrase of 1 Pet. 1:4: εἰς κληρονομίαν ἄφθαρτον καὶ ἀμίαντον καὶ ἀμάραντον. Given the contrast between the vocabulary (hardly the material of everyday speech) and the semi-literate character of the document (phonetic spelling, etc.), the author was probably using some expression he had overheard such as 1 Pet. 1:4.

4-5 Cf. *Pap.Graec.Mag.* II P 15b.8, Θεοτόκε, ἄφθαρτε, ἀμίαντε, ἀμόλυντε.

The Coptic equivalents of both ἀμίαντος and ἄφθαρτος (ⲁⲧⲧⲱⲗⲙ or ⲁⲑⲱⲗⲙ and ⲁⲧⲧⲁⲕⲟ) are both in the present Coptic funeral liturgy, not far from a reference to resting in the bosoms of Abraham, Isaac, and

Jacob; see the offices for the dead, *Pigiom nte Nihibi* (Cairo 1905) 22, 32-34 and a translation in *Coptic Offices,* trans. R. M. Woolley (London 1930) 113, 115-6.

5 ἄφθαρτ ` ε ΄ λέησων. The epsilon is written over the lambda of ἐλέησων; it is unclear whether it is serving as the final epsilon of ἄφθαρτε, the first of ἐλέησων, or both. The scribe appears to have written ἄφθαρτλ, then stopped, wrote the epsilon over the lambda, then continued.

6-8 may be linked with each other. Δεόμεθα, δεσπότης, and οὐράνιος (in the form of its virtual synonym, ἐπουράνιος) are all very common in the early liturgies. It is easy to imagine some prayer like σε δεόμεθα, δέσποτα ἐπουράνιε which may have suggested itself to the writer.

8 Οὐράνιος itself is not an uncommon word, but the vocative, addressed to God, is rarely used in the theological or liturgical literature (the present liturgy of St. John Chrysostom is an exception). It is rare in the Septuagint, and is used there only once as an adjective of God (κύριος ὁ οὐράνιος, 1 Esdras 6: 14). The phrase ὁ πατὴρ ὁ οὐράνιος is used several times in Matthew, but is peculiar to the first Gospel.

9 It is especially difficult to determine what was in the writer's mind when he wrote this line. The text is probably meant to be something like ὦ χορηγήσων πεινῶσι, "O supplier to the hungry." The author either could not choose between omicron and omega, or failed to strike out the omega after making the correction, then forgot to add the eta between the rho and gammma. Χορηγέω is not found in the Gospels. Compare 2 Cor. 9:10: ὁ δὲ ἐπιχορηγῶν σπέρμα τῷ σπείροντι καὶ ἄρτον εἰς βρῶσιν χορηγήσει καὶ πληθυνεῖ τὸν σπόρον ὑμῶν, 1 Pet. 4:11: ὡς ἐξ ἰσχύος ἧς χορηγεῖ ὁ θεός and Gregory Nazianzus, *De Pace 1* (PG35.744b): πεινῶσι δὲ οὐρανὸς ἐχορήγει τροφὴν.

9-13 ὦ I have given the author the benefit of the doubt and kept the omega as an interjection, something not uncommon in addressing deities. However, it could as easily be a phonetic misspelling of ὁ.

11-13 The original form of the phrase, Ἐγώ εἰμι ὁ Θεὸς τοῦ πατρός σου, Θεὸς Αβρααμ καὶ Θεὸς Ισαακ καὶ Θεὸς Ιακωβ (LXX Ex. 3:6), recurs with slight variations several times in the New Testament (Matt. 22:32, Mark 12:26, Luke 20:37, Acts 3:13, 7:32), and is found in magic (*Pap.Graec.Mag.* 1231). It frequently appears in the early liturgical sources, e.g., 11 times in the *Apostolic Constitutions.*

11 The use of 'Αβραάμ as a *nomen sacrum* is exceptional. The name Abraham was spelled several ways in Greek—usually 'Αβραάμ (indeclinable), but also "Αβραμος, 'Αβράμης, and in one fragment from the second century ἀπὸ 'Αβράμωνος: see *A Greek-English Lexicon of the New Testament and Other Early Christian Literature*, ed. W. F. Arndt and F. W. Gingrich, 2nd ed. rev. (Chicago 1979) s.v. I have found only two instances of its possible use as a *nomen sacrum*, both of them irregular and uncertain. One, *P.Bodmer* VII 12.14, is 'Αβραάμ with Σαρρα, which together "are not abbreviations and the superscript line may indicate not so much a *nomen sacrum* as the presence of a non-Greek word," C. H. Roberts, *Manuscript* 39 n. 5. The other, in a text of Melito of Sardis (*P.Bodmer* VIII 49.12), has in one line ἐπὶ τὸν 'Αβραάμ ἀπὸ τοῦ Αβρμ. Since the next line has Ιακοβ, this certainly represents a momentary lapse and not a regular practice. The author of **294** was applying a vaguely understood principle and not an established practice.

295. Fragment of a Homily?

Inv. 455b | 4.6 x 4 cm. | III/IV
Pl. 3 | | Provenance unknown

The papyrus is a small fragment of a previously unknown piece of literature, with text on both sides. One side has an allusion to the sixth chapter of Genesis, while the other refers to the second chapter of John. There is a crease near the middle and several small holes, but the text is not difficult to make out for the most part. The edges are fairly straight, which together with the crease suggests that the papyrus was folded, perhaps several times. Since there seems to be no particular reason for preserving this piece (say as an amulet) it probably broke off and its survival is due to chance. The text on each side runs in the opposite direction to the other, i.e., one side reads upside down in respect to the other; since the hand is the same on both sides, this suggests that the piece was short enough to require only a single page. The early and marked preference within the early Christian community for the codex over the roll makes it unlikely that this piece formed part of a longer treatise covering two sides of a roll.[19] The content gives no certain indication which side was written first. The only way to determine recto and verso is the direction of the fibres in relation to the text.

While the text is clearly a work of literature, the hand is not a literary hand. It resembles, in some ways closely, *P.Beatty* IV (*Pap.* V), dated to the last part of the 3rd century, or at latest to the early 4th, and described by its first editor, Frederic Kenyon, as "non-literary."[20] The

---

[19] See most recently H. Y. Gamble, *Books and Readers in the Early Church* (New Haven 1995) 42-81.

[20] " . . . markedly different from those of all others in the collection, in being of a definite non-literary type. It is a good documentary hand, to which many parallels can be found among the non-literary papyri . . . (its) characteristics will be recognized as belonging to a style of writing which makes its appearance in documents of the third century." F. G. Kenyon, *The Chester Beatty Biblical Papyri*

two hands give the same general impression, though **295** is not as carefully written, and the formation of many of the letters is virtually the same: the well-rounded mu and omega, the deeply-forked upsilon, the two-stroke epsilon, the over-turned sigma, etc. The one clear difference is the odd manner in which the hand of **295** formed -ων and -αν in several cases, where the nu looks as though it had been turned around and ligatured to the preceding omega or alpha.[21] Like the Chester Beatty papyrus, **295** shows the occasional rough breathing with a large curved stroke, as well as diaeresis over initial iota and upsilon. I would place it, too, in the late 3rd century, or perhaps the early 4th.

The recto contains four instances of *nomina sacra*. Two are for Θεός. One is for the genitive plural of men, ἀν(θρώπ)ων, contracted here even though the word is used in a profane, rather than sacred, sense.[22] Most interesting is the contraction κ(όσ)μον. Κόσμος is not one of the fifteen standard *nomina sacra*,[23] being found in contracted form in only two other papyri. One is *P.Lond.* VI 1927.32, a letter from the mid-4th century. The other is*P.Oxy.* VII 1008.36, 40, 44, a fragment of 1 Cor. 7 and 8, which also abbreviates ἄνθρωπος when used in a profane sense. While there are a number of instances of words other than the usual fifteen being treated as *nomina sacra*, most of these have been found only once or twice. Paap, in his study of *nomina sacra*, suggested that the two previously known examples of κόσμος were "probably used under the influence of the story of creation."[24] However, although three cases are still too few to establish anything definite, if any more instances of κόσμος contracted are discovered, then perhaps its use as a *nomen sacrum*

Fasciculus iv, *Genesis* (Pap. V) Plates (London 1936) ix-x; plates are also in Seider, *Paläographie* 2: 141 no. 53, plate 27; B. M. Metzger, *Manuscripts of the Greek Bible* (New York 1981) no. 11.

21 Several, but not all. On the development of nu, see J. P. Gumbert, "Structure and forms of the letter ν," *Studia Papyrologica Varia*, Papyrologica Lugduno-Batava XIV (Leiden 1965) 1-9. The odd ligatured nu here resembles none of Gumbert's examples.

22 *P. Beatty* IV (*Pap.* V) abbreviates κύριος even when used in a profane sense. Kenyon, ix.

23 See Metzger 36-7.

24 Paap, *Nomina Sacra* 114-5; his suggestion is odd, since κόσμος is used only once in the first two chapters of Genesis, γῆ being much more common. A better candidate would be the opening chapter of John. Also on eccentric and unusual forms of *nomina sacra*, K. Aland, ed., *Repertorium der Griechischen Christlichen Papyri, I: Biblische Papyri:* Patristische Texte und Studien 18 (Berlin 1976) 420-8; Roberts, *Manuscript* 39 and 83f; Metzger 37. I have found no other instances of κόσμος as a *nomen sacrum* since Paap's publication.

was not simply an inspiration of the individual writer, but a more serious and widespread *ballon d'essai* for inclusion within the select group.

Lines 5 and 6 of the recto contain the words ὁ Θεὸς φασὶν εἶπεν [±?]ου ἥκει ἐνωπίον μου, which echo a phrase from Genesis 6:13, καὶ εἶπεν ὁ Θεὸς πρὸς Νωε, Καιρὸς παντὸς ἀνθρώπου ἥκει ἐναντίον μου, from the story of the flood.[25] The letters]ωε at the beginning of line 4 would fit nicely with Νωε, the Greek spelling for Noah, while the reference to wrath, ὀργή, certainly makes sense in the context of God's impending destruction of mankind. If the μέλλων of line 4 refers forward to God on line 5, then the φ[that follows presumably refers to God's future intentions and could be the beginning of some verb such as φθείρω (cf. the use of καταφθείρω, Gen. 6:13-14). The resulting reconstruction of lines 4 through 6 makes the average line about 30 letters long (see the commentary below).

If the reference to Genesis 6 on the recto seems probable, the reference on the verso to John 2, the wedding at Cana, is unmistakable. 'Αρχιτρικλίνος is a rare word, not often found outside the Cana wedding story, while the phrase from line 5 is a direct quotation from John 2:9, τὸ ὕδωρ οἶνον γεγενημένον. The only obvious element connecting the two stories, other than their appearance in the Bible, is water.[26] Further consideration shows, however, two possible connections, not mutually exclusive.

The first is the sacrament of baptism. The story of the flood, Noah, and the ark, is used as a "type" of baptism as early as the New Testament (1 Pet. 3:18-22). It is almost always found in lists of Old Testament foreshadowings and other symbols of the sacraments, such as in Tertullian, *De Baptismo* 8-9; Didymus, *De Trinitate* 2.14 (PG39.692-7); Ambrose, *De Sacramentis* 1.23, *De Mysteriis* 24.[27] Surprisingly, the Cana story, too, while usually interpreted eucharistically by the Fathers, was

---

[25] Since the writer is paraphrasing from memory, rather than quoting precisely, the substitution of ἐνωπίον for ἐναντίον is quite natural, the former being much more common in later Greek; it is used commonly and exclusively in the New Testament.

[26] See J. Gaillard, "Eau," in *Dictionnaire de Spiritualité* 4:8-29.

[27] See J. Daniélou, *Sacramentum Futuri: Études sur les origines de la typologie baptismale* (Paris 1950) 77-83; J. Daniélou, *The Bible and the Liturgy* (Notre Dame 1956) 75-85; P. Lundberg, *La typologie baptismale dans l'Ancienne Eglise*, Acta Seminarii Neotestamentici Upsaliensis, vol. x (Leipzig and Uppsala 1942).

sometimes seen as a figure of baptism. Tertullian's list of baptismal types, for example, includes the wedding at Cana.[28]

The second connection is the feast of Epiphany (Theophany in the Orthodox Church) on January 6.[29] Today in the Western churches the feast is principally a celebration of the arrival of the Magi, while in the Eastern churches it is almost entirely the baptism of Christ. However, in the ancient Church, depending on precisely when and where you were, the feast on January 6th could be a celebration of 1) the baptism of Christ, 2) the arrival of the Magi, 3) the nativity, 4) the miracle of Cana, or 5) any combination of the four.

It has been suggested, on the basis of a reference towards the end of the *Epistle of Diognetus* (11.3-5), that some kind of unitive feast of Epiphany existed by the late second or early third century. At the end of the second century, Clement of Alexandria wrote that the Basilideans celebrated the baptism of Christ on either January 6 or 11 (*Stromateis* 1.21). It is unclear what connection this had with contemporary or later orthodox practice, but by the end of the fourth century all churches of the East celebrated the baptism of Christ on January 6th. Cassian states that Egypt, by the late fourth century, celebrated both the nativity and the baptism on that day.[30] (*Collationes* 10.2, PL49.820-1) Epiphanius of Salamis reports that the Egyptians of the fourth century commemorated the nativity and the miracle of Cana on the 6th of January (*Adversus Haereses* 51.22, 30).[31] This is still echoed of this in the Coptic liturgical tradition, which celebrates the nativity on January 6 and refers to the 8th of January as the "third day of the Epiphany and the wedding of Cana."[32] And it is remarkable that, certainly no later than the fifth

---

28 Daniélou, *Bible and Liturgy* 221; Lundberg 22-23.

29 For what follows, see J. Lemarié, "Épiphanie," in *Dictionnaire de Spiritualité* 4:863-879; Daniélou, *Bible and Liturgy* 221; Lundberg 18-23; C. Jones *et. al.*, eds., *The Study of Liturgy* , rev. ed. (New York 1992) 466-468; T. J. Talley, *The Origins of the Liturgical Year* (New York 1986) 79-162; F. C. Senn, *Christian Liturgy: Catholic and Evangelical* (Minneapolis 1997) 159-161.

30 See also *MPER* II p. 83ff and *DACL* s.v. "Papyrus" 4:1395-8 by H. Leclerq.

31 Epiphanius also reports that Egyptians celebrated the baptism of Christ in November. Thomas Talley has tried to show that Epiphanius' clear mistake on the date for the Egyptian celebration of the baptism led him to be mistaken again in naming January 6th as the date for the Egyptian celebration of Cana in his day. Yet the evidence shows that in fourth century Egypt, the baptism was celebrated on January 6th and the Cana wedding very shortly after, as Talley himself admits.

32 Lemarié 866-7; Talley 117, 122-3. The phrase is ambiguous; Lemarié understands it to mean that the Epiphany and Cana were celebrated on the same

century and possibly already in the fourth, the Cana wedding did come elsewhere to be associated on January 6th with the baptism and either the birth of Christ or the arrival of the Magi, especially in Gaul, where Eastern liturgical influence was strong.[33]

In commenting on Christ's baptism, as on the subject of baptism generally, the Fathers again made use of the Flood "type," whether in the context of Epiphany or not, e.g., Ps.-Hippolytus, *De Theophania* 7; Ps.-Gregory Thaumaturgus, *Homilia* IV *(in Sancta Theophania)* (PG10.1187); John Chrysostom, *In Matthaeum* (*Homilia* 12.3) (PG57.13-472). We do find, therefore, in connection with the Epiphany feast of January 6th, both in the ancient liturgical tradition and in the Fathers, a conjunction of Noah, the flood, and the wedding at Cana. An ancient Syrian prayer at the blessing of the waters on the eve of the Epiphany begins with a reference to the flood and, after some other Old Testament types, ends with the miracle of Cana and the baptism of Christ.[34] In the West, where the feast was sometimes referred to as that of the *tria miracula* (the birth or arrival of the Magi; the baptism in the Jordan; Cana),[35] the same conjunction can be found in Paulinus of Nola, *Carmina* 27:43-52 (*Poemata* in PL61.649b); Maximus of Turin;[36] and Peter Chrysologus, *Sermo* 160: *Hodie Spiritus sanctus supernatat aquis specie columbae, ut sicut illa colomba Noe nuntiarat diluvium discessisse mundi* . . . and a few lines later, *Hodie Christus initium dat signorum caelestium, dum convertit aquas in vinum* . . .

The nativity was eventually settled on December 25th. In the East, January 6th became almost exclusively the feast of Christ's baptism, while in the West, the tradition of the *tria miracula* has continued in a modified form: January 6, the Magi; first Sunday after, the baptism; second Sunday after, Cana.[37] The origins of this tradition remain a

---

day, while Talley believes it means that Cana was celebrated three days after Epiphany.

33 Lemarié 867; Talley 143-7.

34 Daniélou, *Bible and Liturgy* 221.

35 In Rome, the antiphon for the Benedictus on the feast of the Epiphany says, "Today the Church is united to her heavenly Bridegroom, since, in the Jordan, Christ washes away her sins, the Wise Men run with gifts to the Royal marriage, and the guests are delighted with water changed into wine, alleleuia." Quoted in Daniélou, *Bible and Liturgy* 221.

36 Scattered throughout his sermons and homilies on the Epiphany, rather than in any one place; see the *Homiliae* 17-35 (PL57:259-302), especially 23, 29, 32, 33, and *Sermones* 7-13 (PL57:545-560), especially 11.

37 See, for example, the lectionary of the 1662 English *Book of Common Prayer*, and Year C of the new common lectionary of many American churches, as in the 1979 Episcopal *Book of Common Prayer*.

subject of speculation and dispute; however, **295** (whose author need not have been Egyptian) could be a clue or indication that the unitive nature of the feast was both early and Eastern.

Recto:] . . . . [
[±? τ]ῆς ἀμ̣ε̣λ̣εί̣ας αὐτ̣ῶν καὶ α[±?]
] ̣ εἰς Θ(εὸ)ν· παραφέ̣ρουσι γὰρ [
4 [±? Ν]ωε ὁπηνίκα μ̣έ̣λλων φ[θείρειν τὸν]
[ὅλο]ν κ(όσ)μον ὁ Θ(εὸ)ς, φασίν, εἶπεν̣ [καιρὸς παντὸς]
[ἀν(θρώπ)]ου ἥκει ἐνώπιον μου· ἰδ[ού ±?]
[±? ἠ]δυνήθη τὴν ὀργὴν αὐτ[οῦ ±?]
8]των ἀν(θρώπ)ων εἰ μὴ οπ[

Verso:] . . . . [. . . . .] . . [
] ̣ του τοῖς ἀποστόλοις μ ̣ [
[±? ἁγί]ων γραφῶν παλαιᾶς τε καὶ κ̣[αινῆς ±?]
4]ην ὁ ἀρχιτρικλίνο̣ς τῶν γ[αμῶν ±?]
[±? ἐγεύσ]α̣τω τὸ ὕδορ οἶνον γεγενη̣[μένον ±?]
]πάντα τὰ πρακτ̣ι̣κὰ ὁλῶν [
]σ̣τιας αὐτῶν ὅτι οὐκ ἀσκοὶ ̣ [
8]ε̣λ̣θόντο̣ς . . . . ἀ̣π̣ὸ ὕ̣δ[ατος ±?]

Recto: 3 Θ̅ν̅ 4 rough breathing mark: ὁπηνικα 5 κ̅μ̅ο̅ν̅ Θ̅ς̅
6 papyrus ϊδ[8 α̅ν̅ω̅ν̅
Verso: 5 papyrus ϋδορ = ὕδωρ 7 rough breathing mark: ὁτι
8 papyrus ϋδ[

Recto: 2 α[= ἀδικίας ? Some such negative seems indicated by the preceding ἀμελείας, perhaps referring to the general wickedness of mankind prior to the flood.

4-6 The proposed reconstruction is likely, but hardly certain. I have suggested two words with ten letters for the end of line 4 and two words with twelve letters for the end of line 5; however, the break could have as easily come after the first word in both cases.

5 ὁ Θ(εὸ)ς, φασίν, εἶπε̣ν " . . . God, they say, said . . . "

Verso: 3 This line seems almost certainly to be a reference to the Old and New Testaments, which strengthens the argument that the author is making some deliberate contrast between water or types of feasts in the one and the other. Compare Origen, μαρτύρια τὰ ἐκ τῶν πεπιστευμένων ἡμῖν εἶναι θείων γραφῶν, τῆς τε λεγομένης παλαιᾶς διαθήκης, καὶ τῆς καλουμένης καινῆς, *De principiis* 4.1.1; from the *dubia* of Athanasius, ὡς οὖν εἴρηται ἐν τούτοις πάντα τά τε τῆς παλαιᾶς καὶ τῆς νέας διαθήκης βιβλία, *Synopsis Scriptura Sacrae* 4 (PG28.296a); Cyril of Jerusalem, ταῦτα δὲ διδάσκουσιν ἡμᾶς αἱ θεόπνευσται γραφαὶ τῆς παλαιᾶς τε καὶ καινῆς διαθήκης, *Catecheses* 4.33.

These parallels suggest a restoration of something like τῶν ἁγίων γραφῶν παλαιᾶς τε καὶ καινῆς διαθήκης, except that there is no article τῆς before παλαιᾶς, as in the above parallels. Another possibility would be τῆς διαθήκης τῶν ἁγίων γραφῶν παλαιᾶς τε καὶ καινῆς. However, neither restoration fits in very well with the fragments of letters that remain, and both require a line quite a bit longer than 30 characters.

3-5 I am indebted to the late Morton Smith for the proposed restorations of line 4 and the beginning of line 5.

6 πάντα τὰ πρακτ̣ικὰ. PGL lists several patristic meanings for πρακτικός, including the use as a substantive that "almost = ἄσκησις." In this context, however, it may be related to the reference to the water changed to wine referred to in the previous line and would mean something "all the deeds" or "all the miracles."

7 'Ασκοί, "wine-skins." The word in John 2 is ὑδρία. This may represent a shift to another story or idea. 'Ασκοί, however, is the term used in the synoptic gospels for putting new wine in new wineskins (Matt. 9:17, Mk. 2:22, Luke 5:37-8) and would be in keeping with the suggested theme of old and new covenants (see note above on line 3 of the verso). The letter after ἀσκοὶ *could* be the left stroke of a kappa for καινοί.

8 Perhaps a reference to the baptism in the Jordan. Compare Matthew 3:16, βαπτισθεὶς δὲ ὁ 'Ιησοῦς εὐθὺς ἀνέβη ἀπὸ τοῦ ὕδατος.

296. Byzantine Hymn

Inv. 488	14.8 x 12.5 cm.	VI
Pl. 4		Provenance unknown

Back blank

The papyrus is actually two pieces by the same hand, almost certainly from the same document. Piece (A) is approximately 14.5 centimeters wide and 6.5 centimeters high. Piece (B) is 14.8 centi-meters wide and 6 centimeters high. (A) is the top of a page; there is a space of 3.5 centimeters from the top to the first line of text, leaving room for only three lines of text. (B) comes from somewhere in the middle of a page and almost certainly continues the text of (A). They are identical in style of hand and subject. The text of both is written across the fibres.

(A) is frayed, with portions of papyrus missing from the upper left and lower right corners. If these portions were not missing, it would be almost the same size and shape as (B). (B)'s edges are sharp, and the last line of text has been cut down the middle horizontally. It thus appears that they were both cut to size for some purpose other than preserving the text.

The hand is a clear, plain, sloping uncial, though not polished. It is characterized by extra ink at the beginning and end of many strokes. Punctuation is by points in the middle or near the top of a line. There are accents marks on lines 4 and 8. The hand bears some resemblance to P.Lond.Inv. 1552,[38] edited by H. I. Bell, which must fall between 506 and 585 and is described by Ruth Barbour as the "only datable example of the plain sloping uncial which was probably the working hand used

---

[38] See *P.Lond.* V 1817. Photos of this text have been published in several places; see *P.Lond.Lit.* 98, plate 7; Seider, *Paläographie* 2:165-6, no. 64, plate 35; G. Cavallo and H. Maehler, *Greek Bookhands of the Early Byzantine Period, A.D. 300 - 800* (BICS Supplement 47, London 1987) no. 32a.

before the spread of minuscule in the ninth century."[39] Bell and Barbour place this in the second half of the sixth century. Closer to the hand of **296** are other liturgical papyri: P.Berlin Inv. 1163, judged by Kurt Treu to be fifth/sixth century; P.Berlin Inv. 17612, placed by Treu in the sixth century;[40] *P.Ryl.* I 7, placed in the sixth century by A. S. Hunt. *P.Ryl.* III 468 is a parchment with a hand quite close to ours; it has the same dot-point punctuation, the same ink blobs at the beginning and end of strokes. C. H. Roberts judged this to be a "liturgical fragment" and dated it to the sixth century.

One remarkable text has a hand that bears an especially strong resemblance to ours, *MPER* XVII 13-25 (plates 9-14). The papyrus codex, now in several fragments but originally one text by a single hand, is a collection of liturgical material, including LXX Dan. 3: 52-56 (see below, footnote 50), dated by the editors to the sixth century. **296** is most likely sixth century. However, a later date is certainly possible.[41]

The text appears to be one full strophe and the first line of another of a Byzantine hymn.[42] It is possible that the text of the first strophe is not complete but continues from the bottom of the previous page, since there is no initial + as there is with the beginning of the second strophe. However, the first strophe makes complete sense without supplying additional text, and at eighty syllables is quite long enough.

The earliest form of Greek hymn not based on classical poetic models was the troparion, a prayer composed in the form of a short poem of one, two, or more strophes. This could be sung independently or be inserted into or follow the psalms and canticles chanted at the morning and evening offices. (Confusingly, the same term is used for a single strophe of later hymn forms.) The kontakion, a poetic homily or sermon often cast in dialogue form of about 18 to 30 strophes ending

---

[39] R. Barbour, *Greek Literary Hands: AD 400-1600* (New York 1981) no. 4.

[40] K. Treu, "Neue Berliner Liturgischer Papyri," *APF* 21 (1971) 57-81 and plates 3 and 8.

[41] *P.Stras.* 397 has a hand similar to ours. It is a Coptic text with three lines of Greek containing an invocation and dating formula, originally dated to 535, then re-dated by R. S. Bagnall and K. Worp to 743, *BASP* 15 (1978) 233-46, especially 240-44, but now confidently dated to 843 by L. S. MacCoull, BASP 24 (1987) 63-66. *MPER* XVII 64, plate 44, is also a hymn based on Dan. 3 on parchment with a hand much like ours, dated by the editors to the 7th/8th century.

[42] The initial lines of every strophe of practically every known Greek hymn are collected in alphabetical order in the *Initia hymnorum ecclesiae graecae*, ed. E. Follieri, *Studi e testi* volumes 211-215 (Vactican City 1960-66). Neither line 1 nor line 9 of **296** is to be found there, however.

with the same refrain, originated in the fifth century and was incorporated into the Byzantine liturgy in the sixth century. Only fragments of most kontakia remain (exceptions are the Akathist Hymn and the kontakia of Romanos the Melodist). By the late seventh century, hymn writers preferred the Kanon, a development of the earlier troparion closely connected to, but not identical with, the traditional Biblical canticles.[43]

The canticles (or odes) are a group of Biblical songs used by the church. These were originally fourteen in number but were later combined and reduced to nine in Jerusalem and Constantinople in the sixth century. The nine include, e.g., the song of Moses (Exodus 15:1-19, the first canticle), the song of the three children (LXX Daniel 3:26-45, 52-6, the seventh canticle; LXX Daniel 3:57-88, the eighth canticle), and the Magnificat and Benedictus (Luke 1:46-55, 68-79, the ninth canticle). These were incorporated into the morning office, or Orthros, at some point in the fifth or sixth century.[44] Soon after, brief stanzas or troparia were introduced between the verses of these canticles. There is a report from the sixth century of two monks from Jerusalem, John and Sophronius, who, on a visit to the monastery of Mount Sinai, were shocked at the omission of the troparia from the hymns, psalms, and canticles.[45] These troparia came to be attached to all the nine canticles and increased in number in the seventh and eighth centuries, until they became standardized in the form known as the Kanon, an ode of praise closely modeled on one of the nine canticles. The Kanon could commemorate a saint or celebrate a feast, but it had to refer in some way to the original canticle. Eventually, Kanons replaced the canticles on which they were based in the Orthros.[46]

The invention of the Kanon, at least as a fixed form, is traditionally ascribed to St. Andrew of Crete (c. 660-740). In 1938, C. H. Roberts published *P.Ryl.* III 466, which he dated to the seventh century and which contained two brief hymns apparently attached to the eighth and ninth Canticles. Roberts believed that these were remnants of an early

---

43 E. Wellesz, *A History of Byzantine Music and Hymnography*, 2nd ed., rev. and enl. (Oxford 1961) 171-197.

44 Wellesz 37-8.

45 Wellesz 172-4; text in W. von Christ and M. Paranikas, eds., *Anthologia Graeca Carminum Christianorum* (Leipzig 1871) xxx-xxi. They are almost certainly to be identified with the well-known John Moschus, author of the *Pratum Spirituale*, and Sophronius "the sophist," later Patriarch of Jerusalem. For doubts about this story, see Chitty, *Desert* 170-171.

46 Wellesz 198.

stage of Kanon writing and that this supported the view that the invention of the form pre-dated Andrew, a conclusion repeated by later scholars,[47] perhaps because Wellesz never referred to it in his *History*. However, Wellesz did discuss it in the *Cambridge Medieval History*,[48] where he convincingly contradicted Roberts and placed the hymns in the category of troparia independently attached to the Canticles, such as John and Sophronius expected to hear on Sinai.

Given the probable sixth century date for **296**, this is the most likely category for it as well. Lines 6-8 are clearly based on Daniel 3:53, so the text is probably connected to this Canticle. The occasion for these troparia was probably Lent. The text can be compared with other troparia from Kanons in the Triodion, the lenten service book of the Orthodox church:

Νηστεύσας ὁ Κύριος, τεσσαράκοντα μέτρον ἡμερῶν, τὰς νῦν ἀφιέρωσε, καὶ ἡγίασεν ἡμέρας ἀδελφοί· ἐν αἷς φθάσαντες κράζομεν· Εὐλογεῖτε, καὶ ὑπερυψοῦτε, Χριστὸν εἰς τοὺς αἰῶνας.

Νηστεύσας ὁ Κύριος, ἡμέρας τεσσαράκοντα, ἐν τῇ ἐρήμῳ, ὕστερον ἐπείνασε, δεικνὺς τὸ ἀνθρώπινον. Ψυχὴ μὴ ἀθυμήσῃς· ἄν σοι προσβάλῃ ὁ ἐχθρός, προσευχαῖς τε καὶ νηστείαις, ἐκ ποδῶν ἀποκρουσθήτω σοι. (from the Great Canon of Lent)[49]

In line 9 we find πάνσεπτος. PGL lists only one instance (and an obscure one—see PG87.3160b) where πάνσεπτος is applied to God, in this case the Trinity. All other references in PGL and LSJ are to sanctuaries, feasts, or saints, e.g., the Virgin. The strophe which begins with line 9 may well have been a Theotokion, a troparion in praise of the Virgin. This would follow the text of **296** naturally if the liturgical pattern assumed by **296** followed the earlier pattern of fourteen canticles instead of the later division of nine. In both cases, the canticles taken from Daniel 3 are followed by the Magnificat. However, in the later order, the seventh canticle is LXX Daniel 3: 26-45 and 52-6, while the eighth is verses 57-88; but a more natural division would be 26-45 and 52-88, as in fact was the case when the canticles numbered fourteen. If the local liturgical tradition in which **296** was produced followed the

---

47 van Haelst, *Catalogue* no. 978; Seider, *Paläographie* 2: 177-8, no. 40, plate 40.

48 E. Wellesz, "Byzantine Music and Liturgy," in vol. IV part II of *The Cambridge Medieval History*, ed. J. M. Hussey, 2nd ed., (Cambridge 1967) 147.

49 Texts from *Triodion Katanyktikon* (Athens 1967) 80, 311.

earlier pattern, then this text would be connected with the canticle immediately preceding the Magnificat, and a troparion to the Virgin might well come next.[50]

(A) νηστίαν εὐαρέστων ἀγ[ίαν τῷ Θεῷ]
προσηέγκομεν · καὶ γὰρ αὐ[τὸς]
ἐνήστευσεν ἡμ[έρας τεσσα-]
(B) 4 ράκοντα · νηστίαν μὴ δεόμε-
νος ὁ Θ(εό)ς · ἀλλὰ σοσαι βουλόμενος
τὸ γένος τον ἀν(θρώπ)ων · ὁ ὑπερύμνη-
τος γὰρ εἶ · καὶ ὑπερένδοξον εἰς
8 τος αἰῶνας +
+ τὸν πάσεπτον θῖον ἅγιον

1 νηστίαν = νηστείαν εὐαρέστων = εὐαρέστως or εὐάρεστον
2 προσηέγκομεν = προσηνέγκωμεν 4 νηστίαν = νηστείας
5 $\overline{\Theta\varsigma}$ σοσαι = σῶσαι 6 τον = τῶν $\overline{\alpha\nu\omega\nu}$ 7 ὑπερένδοξον = -δοξος
8 τος = τοὺς 9 πάσεπτον = πάνσεπτον θῖον = θεῖον

Let us bring a holy fast to God in an acceptable manner; for indeed he fasted forty days; God not needing a fast, but intending to save the race of man; for You are highly hymned and greatly glorified unto the ages.

The all-venerable, divine, holy . . .

1 The colons in the transcription correspond to dots in the text. There is also a mark between νηστίαν and εὐαρέστων, but this is

[50] For a list of Marian hymns and prayers in the papyri, see the tabulation by A. M. Emmett in *New Docs 1977* 145-6. It is equally possible that **296** was produced in a church or monastery that followed neither pattern. *MPER* XVII 13-25 is an assortment of liturgical material from a single codex whose principle of organization is unclear (see the review by C. Kuehn in *BASP* 30 (1993) 155-164). Number 15 is the text of Daniel 3: 52-66, identified by editors as the first part of the eighth Kanon (mistakenly—see Wellesz 37). It clearly shows that Daniel 3: 52-66 could stand alone as a liturgical unit in sixth century Egypt.

probably not actually a punctuation mark, but rather stray ink; the others have some space between themselves and the surrounding letters, while this does not. Also, it hardly makes sense, unless we suppose the text to be a continuation from a previous page; but that would leave προσηνέγκωμεν without an object.

The best way to make grammatical sense of the text is to treat the second word of line 1 as an adverb, "in an acceptable manner." This can be done in two ways. One is to substitute an omicron for the ω and read an adverbial accusative. However, although the scribe elsewhere changes omega to omicron several times, he does not change omicron to omega. Another way is to substitute ς for ν and read εὐαρέστως. N for ς may seem an unlikely mistake, but the same error is clearly made in line 4 (νηστίαν for νηστείας) and again in line 7 (-δοξον for -δοξος), and ν is omitted before the σ of πάνσεπτος in line 9. See Gignac, *Grammar* 1.131-132 on the interchange of sigma and nu.

The restoration at the end of line 1 could be ἁγ[ίῳ τῷ Θεῷ]. However, Kurt Treu suggested ἁγ[ίαν τῷ Θεῷ], and a comparison with LXX Joel 1:14 and 2:15, ἁγιάσατε νηστείαν (frequently quoted by the Fathers), supports this. Θεῷ was likely written as a nomen sacrum.

3-4 The last clearly visible letter of line 3 is the beginning of η, followed by faded ink which suggests μ; after this the line fades completely and then breaks off. τεσσα- must certainly precede line 4. ἐνήστευσεν ἡμέρας τεσσαράκοντα makes perfect sense in the context. A stroke extending from the top of (B) into line 4 falls where we would expect to find the downstroke of the ρ of ἡμέρας in line 3.

5-6 ἀλλὰ σοσαι βουλόμενος/ τὸ γένος τον ἀν(θρώπ)ων Cf. τὸ γένος τῶν ἀν(θρώπ)ων, *MPER* XVII 57.6, 14; διὰ βαπτίσματος ἔσωσας τὸ γένος τῶν ἀνθρώπων, Romanos the Melodist II Proemium I (*Sources Chrétiennes* 99, ed. José Grosdidier de Matons); ἵνα τῆς πλάνης σώσῃ ὡς Θεός, τὸ γένος τῶν ἀνθρώπων, *Triodion Katanyktikon* (Athens 1963) 239: τοῦ σῴζοντος τὸ γένος τῶν ἀνθρώπων, *Horologion to Mega* (Athens 1963) 451 (from the Pentacostarion); ὅτι τὸ γένος ἔσωσας τῶν ἀνθρώπων, ibid. 470. Also ὅπως τὸ γένος τῆς ἀνθρωπότητος διὰ σοῦ ὑπὸ Θεοῦ σωθῇ, *Corpus Hermeticum* 1.26 (*Poimandres*).

6-8 The third chapter of LXX Daniel is full of material suitable for inclusion in troparia of all sorts, including those with no special relation to any canticle; see, e.g., nos. 517 and Ad. 39 line 20 in *Coptic Ostraca from the Collection of the Egypt Exploration Fund, the Cairo Museum, and others*, ed. and trans. W. E. Crum and F. M. Brightman (London

1902). However, the style of **296** is so like that of the troparia in the developed Kanon form that a formal connection to the seventh canticle is the most reasonable explanation.

Documentary Texts

297. List Relating to Axles

Inv. 466a	8.4 x 11.3 cm.	V/VI
Pl. 5		Oxyrhynchite nome

The hand of the recto, though cursive, is not difficult to read, but has contractions, ligatures, and odd spelling errors. It looks like a compromise between the need to leave a legible record and a desire to write it out quickly. The few letters on the verso are very neat, clear, and large, with no ligature, though cursive in form, written apparently only to indicate the content on the opposite side.

The document undoubtedly comes under the general heading of "accounts and lists," though exactly what type of account or list is not immediately apparent. Evidently it is concerned with more than one ἄξων, sometimes spelled in the papyri αὔξων and usually translated "axle," a central component of the water-wheel, or μηχανή, and the water-basket, both used for irrigation. The same devices, later called a *sakkieh* and *shaduf* respectively, are still in use in Egypt today. The ἄξων would presumably be the central axle on which the wheel turned.[51]

---

[51] For a description and illustration, see N. Lewis, *Life in Egypt Under Roman Rule* (New York 1983) 113-4 and plate 7; A. K. Bowman, *Egypt After the Pharaohs: 332 BC - AD 642* (California 1986) 19-20 and illustration 10. For a complete study, see J. P. Oleson, *Greek and Roman Mechanical Water-Lifting Devices: The History of A Technology*, Phoenix supplementary volume 16 (Toronto 1984) 370-385, especially 380-5. Oleson believes that the term μηχανή was applied to both the water-wheel and water-basket, and that the ἄξων was not only a central axle for the water-wheel but also the term for the long pole of the water-basket, 381. On irrigation in Greco-Roman Egypt in general, see D. Bonneau, *Le régime administratif de l'eau du Nil dans l'Égypt grécque, romaine et byzantine*, Probleme der Ägyptologie 8 (Leiden 1993), especially 105-115 and 220-234 for the meaning, use, and upkeep of the μηχαναί. See also *P.Berl. Sarischouli* 12, a letter dated to the fourth or fifth century which mentions the shipment of ἄξονες on the Nile.

Such μηχαναί, scattered across the great estates of Egypt of late antiquity, had names,[52] and their upkeep was usually the shared responsibility of the landlord and an individual *colonus*. Ματρῖνος is the name of one such water-wheel (*P.Oxy.* XIX 2244.59) near Oxyrhynchus on the Apion estates. Since the name appears on this document, and since the Apions were probably the largest land-holders of the fifth and sixth centuries in Egypt, and those for whom we have the most extensive documentation, this papyrus is quite possibly, though far from certainly, from the Apion archives.[53] Some documents as early as the second century AD mention both μηχαναί and ἄξονες, but the huge majority of accounts mentioning both are from the fifth to seventh centuries, and *P.Oxy.* LVIII 3960 shows the Apion household was still operating as late as 621 under the Persians. Dating something this fragmentary is therefore admittedly an educated guess.

P.Oxy. XIX 2244 (6th/7th century) is a list of "axles supplied for the water-wheels, installed in the various estates of the Apion family." There are six columns, a total of 90 lines, describing the distribution of axles across the enormous estates to the various *coloni* for the water-wheels of which they were in charge, with line after line listing the name of the *colonus* (in the dative), his hamlet (ἐποίκιον) or village (κώμη), the name of the water-wheel he served and the number of axles supplied. Additional information is given, including sometimes the source of supply, for example ἐκ τῶν ἐνεχθέντων νῦν, ἐκ τῶν ἐνεχθέντων ἀπ' Ἀλεξανδρείας, or ἐκ τῶν ἐκκλησίας.[54]

There are also many receipts from *coloni* for axles or other parts.[55] These follow a standard formula. The *colonus* who requires the part approaches the landlord, who orders someone to supply it. This someone can be the steward (οἰκέτης- *P.Oxy.* XXXVI 2779); in a case where the property belongs to the principal church of Oxyrhynchus and the landlord is the bishop, a monk (*P.Oxy.* XVI 1900 of 528 AD); a τέκτων (*P.Oxy.* XVI 1899 of 476 AD); or a μηχανουργός (*P.Oxy.* XVI 1987 of 587 AD). The *colonus* could also purchase an axle himself "in the fields" and be reimbursed by the estate (*P.Oxy.* XVI 1911.160-4, 169-74 of 557 AD; *P.Oxy.* XVI 1988-1991 of 587, 590, 591, 616 AD respectively).

---

52 Bonneau 221.

53 On the Apions and the Apion archives, see E. R. Hardy, *The Large Estates of Byzantine Egypt* (New York 1931) 25-38 and Jean Gascou, "Les grands domaines, la cité et l'état en Égypte byzantine," *T&MByz* (1985) 9: 61-75.

54 On this and other such lists, see Bonneau 230-234.

55 Hardy 127-8; Bonneau 226-230.

297 does not correspond to any of the above, though it deals with the same subject matter and uses similar formulas. It therefore most likely reflects axles *received* by the estate, whether by purchase or other obligation (cf. the information on sources of supply quoted from *P.Oxy.* XIX 2244 above). The list could be an inventory, giving the source, number, and perhaps an intended destination (line 4). This would help make sense of line 2; it is difficult to see how else a πραγματευτής could make his way onto such a list.

If this hypothesis is correct, then, since we already possess receipts for, and records of the distribution of, axles, **297** is a hitherto unattested link in the chain of an important part of estate management. A partial parallel might be *P.Oxy.* LVIII 3960, the account of a wine steward in charge of one area of the Apion estates in 621; he lists quantities of wine actually received through obligation (column one) and purchase (column two), followed then by quantities disbursed as gifts, payments, or requisitions (column three), and quantities still owed to the estate (column four).

What can be determined about the individuals listed? The most likely translation for πραγματευτής is "business representative" or "trader" (see note), which makes it more likely that the document represents axles acquired by the estate. The γεωργός of line 8 is from an ἐποίκιον, presumably a tenant on an estate (given the nature of the document), and could be a *colonus adscripticius* (γεωργός ἐναπόγραφος),[56] possibly connected with the Apion estates.

Lower clergy worked for the major estates in many capacities, from γεωργός (e.g., *P.Oxy.* XIX 2244.89) to προνοητής (*P.Oxy.* I 136).[57] They were also engaged in skilled labor to support themselves and were so encouraged by the Church, which could not afford to support them and their families entirely out of its own resources.[58] The two deacons

---

56 Hardy 132-3; Jones, *Later Roman Empire* 795-803. Our view of the origins and prevalence of the colonate has been much debated in recent years; see J.-M. Carrié, "Le 'Colonat du Bas-Empire': une mythe historiographique?" *Opus* 1 (1982) 351-370; "Un roman des origines: les généalogies du 'Colonat du Bas-Empire'," *Opus* 2 (1983) 205-251; Figures du 'Colonat' dans les papyrus d'Égypte: lexique, contextes," *Atti des XVII Congresso Internazionale di Papirologia* III (Naples 1984), 939-948; Gascou 20-27; Bagnall, *Egypt* 115; I. F. Fikhman, "De nouveau sur le colonat du Bas Empire," *Miscellanea Papyrologica* (*Papyrologica Florentina* XIX) (Firenze 1990) 159-179; Miroslava Mirkovic, *The Later Roman Colonate and Freedom* (Philadelphi 1997).

57 Wipszycka, *Ressources* 161; Hardy 140 and the papyri cited there.

58 Wipszycka, *Ressources* 156-7, 163-5.

here are listed according to their ἐποίκια and may have been *coloni adscripticii*, something that was not necessarily a bar to holy orders.[59]

The case of the monk is more interesting. There is evidence for large numbers of monks in and around places such as Oxyrhynchus by the fifth century, under the control of the local bishop.[60] By the end of the fifth century, the church of Oxyrhynchus controlled a fair amount of land administered by the bishop or subordinates, with monks assisting in the management (*P.Oxy.* XVI 1896, 1900). The Apions had extensive relations with the Church and the monasteries. Their estates received axles ἐκ τῆς ἐκκλησίας (*P.Oxy.* XIX 2244) and purchased products of the monasteries (*P.Oxy.* I 148, *P.Oxy.* XVI 2015).[61] Monks would come in from their desert monasteries to work as day-laborers in the Delta during harvest time,[62] though day labor rarely left any trace in the papyrus record.[63] To judge from the Nepheros archive and comments by Jerome, some monks of the fourth century not easily classed as either eremitic or cenobitic were individually involved in commerce and continued to own and cultivate land and other private properties.[64]

The monk of **297** does not fit into any of these categories. If the restoration at the end of line 5 is correct, then he is listed as from an ἐποίκιον, not a monastery, and hence is likely to have been a *colonus*. This is particularly so if he was connected in any way with the water-wheel mentioned on the next line.

To date I have not located another monk identified as either a μονάζων or μόναχος and serving as a *colonus*. However, in *P.Oxy.* XVIII 2195, an account of receipts from and expenditure on estates of the Apions, and *P.Oxy.* XVIII 2197, an account of bricks collected and then distributed for the Apion estates, some of the tenants are listed as πρεσβύτερος, and at least one is listed as ἄπα ˀΩρ γεωργ(οῦ) (καὶ) πρεσβ(υτέρου), 2197.162, while seven are listed only as ἄπα so-and-so or in one case ἄπα ˀΩρ γ[εωργ(οῦ). At least some, and probably all, of the "Apas" were unordained monks, unattached to a monastery and working as tenants. They may even have been adscripts, since retiring to

---

59 *Codex Justinianus* 1.3.16, 36; *Novellae* 123.4, 17; Hardy 140; Jones, *Later Roman Empire* 802, 920-2; Mirkovic 80. The only way out of adscript status was, under Justinian, by becoming a bishop.

60 *Historia Monachorum* 5; Chitty, *Desert* 24-5.

61 Hardy 128-9, 140-2.

62 Chitty, *Desert* 34, 145.

63 Bagnall, *Egypt* 123.

64 For the secular activities of monks, see the introduction to *P.Neph.* pages 17-20, and in particular *P.Neph.* 12. See also the introduction to **299** below.

a monastery was no means of escaping such obligations. By 452 (or at least 484 in the east), the *adscripticii* were forbidden to enter monasteries without their landlord's consent. Justinian ruled that if someone did enter a monastery and his status were uncertain, he could only be accepted tentatively for three years; if anyone came to claim him in that time as an *adscripticius*, he had to return.[65]

Given the large numbers of monks and the extent of the estates in Egypt, including in and around Oxyrhynchus, it is not improbable that a *colonus* might have declared his desire to live as a monk and yet remained bound to the land. Alternatively, he might have left, joined a monastery, and been reclaimed later, still considered a monk (at least in his own mind) but resuming his former status. The imperial legislation indicates that there must have been a problem, as does the statement of the emperor Marcian to the council of Chalcedon in 451 that slaves and adscripts could not be received in monasteries without the knowledge of their masters.[66]

Recto: [±12] α̣ὔ̣[ξων ±?]
Λε[ο]ν̣τ̣ίου πραγματευτοῦ [
Παύλου διακόν(ου) ἀπὸ ἐποκ(ίου) Φ[
εἰς τὴν μηναχὴν καλο[υ]μ̣[ένην ±?]
῾Ηρακλεις μονάζον ἀπὸ τ[οῦ αὐτοῦ ±?]
Ματρίνου αὔξωνα ἕνα
᾿Ανουτίου διακόνου ἀπὸ ἐποι̣[κίου ±?]
[Πα]ῆσις γεωργ(οῦ) ἀπὸ ἐποκίου κ̣[
[. .] . [. .] . . . . . ἀπὸ κώμης . [
± 15 ἀ]πὸ ἐποικ[(ίου) ±?]
± 18 αὔ]ξωνα[

Verso (with the fibres):]β̣ρ(έουιον) ἄξώνω̣[ν

[65] *Codex Justinianus* 1.3.36, 37; *Novellae* 35.3, 123.35; Jones, *Later Roman Empire* 931.

[66] *Acta Conciliorum Oecumenicorum*, ed. E. Schwartz, II: *Concilium Universale Chalcedonense* (Berlin 1933) 1.2 §17 page [353] 157.

There is some additional text in a different hand, very small, fragmentary, faded, and no longer legible, extending from the left edge and written across the fibres of the verso.

1 αὔξων = ἄξων 3 ἐποκ// = ἐποικ(ίου) 4 μηναχὴν = μηχανὴν
5 'Ηρακλεις = 'Ηρακλῆς μονάζον = μονάζων or perhaps μονάζον(τος)
6, 11 αὔξωνα = ἄξωνα 7 διακόνου corr. from διακ/
8 ἐποκίου = ἐποικίου 10 ἐποικ/
Verso Βρ/

2 πραγματευτοῦ. "Business representative," Latin *actor*, acting on behalf of the Apions, seems the most likely translation, rather than "official"; see *NewDocs 1977* 60-1, no. 19, and J.–J. Aubert, *Business Managers in Ancient Rome* (Leiden 1994) 186-196. Aubert's evidence is Italian and only covers to AD 250. However, by the date of this papyrus, another strong possibility is "trader," an independent businessman; compare with *P.Oxy.* XVI 1880, note 5; *P.Oxy.* XVI 1881, 2058; *P.Cair.Masp.* II 67158.17; Palladius, *Historia Lausiaca* 13 (14 in PG34.1035); and see the notes to P.Col.Inv. 441 by W. L. Westermann, "Entertainment in the villages of Graeco-Roman Egypt," *JEA* 18 (1932) 16-7 (the text has been re-published as *P.Col.* VIII 226).

3 I have found only one other deacon listed in estate documents of a similar nature, *P.Oxy.* XIX 2244.89-90: 'Απολλῷ διακόν(ῳ) καὶ 'Ιωσηφ 'Ιωάννου γεωρ(γοῖς) ἀπὸ κώμ(ης) εἰς χρείαν τῆς μηχ(ανῆς)/ καλουμ(ένης) Μαρίας Θωθ κη ἰνδ(ικτ.) ζ ἄξ(ων) α.

4 μηναχήν. This can hardly be a case of phonetic interchange. Instead, the metathesis witnesses to the hurried nature of the document. See Gignac, *Grammar* I: 59, 154.

6 The line appears to end with a flourish at the end of ἕνα followed by a space and no indication of any text extending beyond the right edge of the papyrus.

298. Christian Letter

Inv. 148 | 14 x 18 cm. | III/IV
Pl. 6 | | Provenance unknown

The papyrus is badly damaged, with many holes and a large gash down the center, so that a considerable portion of the text has been lost. The text is more or less complete for lines 13 - 16 only. It breaks off after line 17, but as this appears to be the beginning of the final greeting, probably only a few lines are missing. The verso has the remains of an address written with a neater, larger hand.

The hand is semi-cursive, with frequent ligatures, but not difficult to read where the condition of the papyrus permits. With no discernible tilt to left or right, it resembles to a degree *P.Alex.* 29, dated to the 3rd/4th century. The editor of *P.Alex.* 29 compared that hand to Schubart, *Pap.Gr.Berol.* 34a, dated 203; **298** also bears some resemblance, especially as regards upsilon, eta, and delta. I would place it in the late 3rd or early 4th century.

The text exhibits some features in common with Christian letters of peace, ἐπιστολαὶ εἰρηνικαί, long known from canons eleven and thirteen of the council of Chalcedon and earlier canons as well (and not to be confused with letters of recommendation, ἐπιστολαὶ συστατικαί).[67] These short, stereotyped letters were intended to provide their humble lay bearer with material support while travelling. At least ten of these have been published by now and their form has been carefully

[67] See T. M. Teeter, "Letters of Recommendation or Letters of Peace?" *Akten des 21. Internationalen Papyrologenkongresses* (Stuttgart, Leipzig 1997) 954-960. On letters of recommendation in general, see *Epistolographi Graeci*, ed. R. Hercher (Paris 1873) 8; C. W. Keyes, "The Greek Letter of Introduction," *AJP* 56 (1935) 28-44; Kim, *Familiar Letter* with 83 examples from published sources; Montevecchi, *La Papirologia* 243; White, *Ancient Letters* 193-194, 203-204 and nos. 11, 71, 77-79, 115a; S. K. Stowers, *Letter Writing in Greco-Roman Antiquity* (Philadelphia 1986) 153-165.

analysed.[68] They are nearly identical in their content, wording, order, and brevity, differing from each other only in minor details. They have unique features, such as the phrase (κατὰ τὸ ἔθος, ὡς καθήκει, or ἐν εἰρήνῃ) accompanying a δέχομαι-compound. Two of them (*SB* X 10255 = Naldini no. 20, *PSI* IX 1041 = Naldini no. 29) mention catechumens. For example:

***PSI* III 208**

Χ̣αῖρε ἐν κ(υρί)ῳ, ἀγαπητὲ
[ἄδ]ελφε Πέτρε, Σώτ̣[ας]
σε προσαγορεύω.
Τ̣ὸν ἀδελφὸν ἡμῶν
Ἡ̣ρακλῆν παράδεξαι
[κ]ατὰ τὸ ἔθος, δι' οὗ σὲ
καὶ τοὺς σὺν σοὶ πάν-
τας ἀδελφοὺς ἐγὼ
κ̣αὶ οἱ σὺν ἐμοὶ
προσαγορεύομεν.
ἐρρῶσθαι σε
ἐν Θ(ε)ῷ εὔχομαι.

***P.Oxy.* LVI 3857**

τοῖς κατὰ τόπον ἀγαπητοῖς
ἀδελφοῖς καὶ συνλειτουργοῖς
τὴν θυ̣γ̣α̣τέρα ἡμῶν Γερ-
μανίαν, ἐπικουρίας
δεομένην, π[αραγι-
νομένην πρὸς
ὑμᾶς προσδέξασθε
ἐν εἰρηνῃ, δι'ἧς
ὑ̣μᾶς καὶ τοὺς σὺν
ὑμῖν ἐγώ τε καὶ οἱ σὺν
ἐμοὶ προσαγορεύ-
ομεν. 'Εμ(μανουή)λ. ϙθ
ἐρρῶσθαι ὑμᾶς
ἐν κυρίῳ εὔχομαι,
ἀγαπητοὶ ἀδ̣ε̣λφοι̣.

Other letters appear to have picked up features of these letters of peace, such as:

68 Kim, *Familiar Letter* 99-118; K. Treu, "Christliche Empfehlungs-Schemabriefe auf Papyrus" in *Zetesis. Bijdragen . . . E. de Strijcker* (Antwerp/Utrecht 1973) 629-636; Tibilletti, *Lettere Private* 102-4. Most recently, see *P.Oxy.* 3857. Not included by either Treu or or the editor of *P. Oxy.* 3857 (M. G. Sirvianou) is *P.Oxy.* XLIII 3149, which clearly echoes the stereotyped form, but departs from it in some respects, whether because of the author's lack of education, the late date, or the nature of the recipient (probably a monk).

• *P.NagHamm.* 77. 4th century. This fragment of a letter passes on the recommendation of a bishop and refers to other matters besides. It contains some of the features of a letter of peace.

• *P.NagHamm.* 78. 4th century. This fragment of a letter opens in the same manner as a letter of peace, and by line 6 (shortly before it breaks off) appears to pick up this simple model again. However, the body of the text show an elaboration not found in the simple letter of peace, which always begins with τὸν ἀδελφὸν, κατηχούμενον, or something similar. Instead, in lines 3 to 6 we find ἐν πρώτοις ἀναγκαῖο[ν ἡγησάμην] προσειπεῖν σου τὴν ἔμ[φυτον ἀγά]πην, ἔπειτα καὶ γράφειν [σοι ἵνα] προσδέξῃ τὸν ἀδελφὸν [ἡμῶν] *κτλ.* The writer has augmented the basic model of a letter of peace.

• *P.Oxy.* XXXI 2603, first edited by J. H. Harrop,[69] 4th century. A close look shows that it is related to the letter of peace.[70] The first 19 lines contain a self-consciously literary discourse on mirrors, ending with "For as through a mirror you have seen τὴν πρὸς σέ μου ἔ[μ]φυτον στοργὴν καὶ ἀγάπην τὴν ἀεὶ νέαν," followed shortly by ἀναγκαῖ]ον μοί ἐστιν γράψαι ⟦σοι⟧ (line 22) (underlining mine).[71] Compare this with the lines from *P.NagHamm.* 78 quoted above. Then, in lines 24ff., after a reference to τοὺς ἡμετέρους ἀδελφούς, the recipient is asked πρόσδεξαι οὖν ἐν ἀγάπῃ, clearly an echo of the δέχομαι-compound plus short phrase found in a letter of peace. The beginning of the final greeting resembles that of the letter of peace, including the use of προσαγορεύω. A note in the left-hand margin (possibly in a different hand) refers to writing more such letters as if this were a general practice and uses both the δέχομαι-compound and the phrase κατὰ τόπον found in several letters of peace. All this suggests that *P.Oxy.* XXXI 2603 is an adaptation of the letter of peace with a lengthy "literary" preamble.

Thus both *P.NagHamm.* 78 and *P.Oxy.* 2603 are expansions of this simple letter of peace, or at least show a literary dependence. *P.Oxy.* XXXI 2603 may even be an expansion of something like *P.NagHamm.* 78, if the parallels between them mean anything. **298** contains a

---

69 J. H. Harrop, "A Christian Letter of Commendation," *JEA* 48 (1962) 133-40; see also Naldini, *Cristianesimo* no. 47.

70 This was clearly understood by Treu 635-6; see also Harrop's note on line 25, and Kim 113 n. 24.

71 Naldini accepts a suggestion of οὐ δέον instead of ἀναγκαῖον. I prefer Harrop.

recommendation and is too long to be following the short form of a letter of peace. Could it also be a expansion of the letter of peace?

The body of the letter, though badly damaged, does not at first encourage such a conclusion. The text contains several words and expressions (ἀσφαλίζω, μελέτη, θεία ἄσκησις, κάκωσις, θειότης, κτλ.) which belong to the realm of Christian doctrine and spiritual discipline, the vocabulary of sanctification, rather than to any straightforward transaction between two people or communities or to an appeal to the recipient's good nature (see notes and PGL s.v.). In addition, where the letter is readable and where it most clearly resembles a letter of peace (lines 14-17), the name of the person recommended, in this case a catechumen, is not given precisely where we would expect to find it (although the persons recommended in *P.Oxy.* 2603 are not named either). On the other hand, there are two points which remind us of the letter of peace: the request to receive the catechumen using a δέχομαι-compound and the final greeting to the brethren with προσαγορεύσατε which immediately follows.

Given the extensive lacunae, we cannot be certain of the occasion and purpose of **298**, but it may well be a letter of peace with a spiritual (rather than literary) preamble, perhaps of a consolatory or hortatory nature (note the προτρέπω of line 11).[72] Such an exhortation would be particularly appropriate in the case of the catechumen of line 15, unbaptized, unformed, perhaps not even very deeply instructed.[73]

---

72 For the genre, see Stowers, *Letter Writing* ch. 10; a contemporary pagan example is *P.Oxy.* XLII 3069 (Stowers 99); a Christian example is *P.Oxy.* XVI 1874.

73 On the early history of the catechumenate, see M. Dujarier, *A History of the Catechumenate: The First Six Centuries*, trans. E. J. Haasl (New York 1979) and Robert Grant, "Development of the Christian Catechumenate" in *Made, Not Born: New Perspectives on Christian Initiation and the Catechumenate* (Notre Dame 1976) 32-49. Among older works: *DACL* s.v. "Catéchèse-Catéchisme-Catéchumene" 2:2530-2579 and "Catéchumenat" 2:2579-2621, still very good. In this period one remained a catechumen for at least two or three years, often for life.

Recto: Θωμᾶς κ̣α̣ὶ̣ [. . .] . μ̣α̣ς̣ καὶ ο̣ἱ̣ σὺ̣ν̣ ἡ̣[μῖν] π̣ά̣ν̣τ̣ε̣ς̣
Π̣α̣ύ̣λ̣ῳ̣ τ̣ῷ̣ [. . . .] . . . ιωτ̣ . . . .
. . . πε . [.]ο̣ι̣σ̣ . [. . πλ]εῖ[σ]τα [χα]ίρειν.
ἐ̣π̣ειδὴ τ̣ου[. . . . .]ν̣τ̣κ̣α̣ . . . ν . . ελ̣ε-
ξαμεν ε̣πε . δ̣[. . . . . .] πρ̣ὸς ὑ̣μ̣ᾶ̣ς ἀσπάσασθαί
σε π̣ρο . [.] . . . . . [. . . . .]εως ἀ̣σφαλείσητε περὶ
τ̣ὸ τη . [. . .]φ̣ον κ . [. . . . .] . . [.] καὶ περὶ τὴ[ν] με-
λέτην̣ κ̣αὶ [τ]ὴ̣ν . . . . [. .] ὑ̣μ̣ῶν θείαν ἄσκησι⟨ν⟩·
Θ̣ε̣ὸς δ̣[ὲ] πα̣[.]ας καὶ . . υμ[ε]ῖ̣ν̣ ἐ̣ν πᾶσι βοηθῶν
τοῦ δια̣[. . . . . .] . εμου̣σ[. .] . . . α̣ν τῆς κ[α]κώσε-
ῳ̣ς τοὺς διδ . . [.]σ[.]συ[. . .] . . ων καὶ προτρέπω
επιπ̣αρ . θον[.] . [. . .] . [. . . .] . . . δε τῆι μελέτηι
καὶ τῆι θει[ότ]ητι μέχ̣ρις οὗ τέλεον τῆς
ἀναπαύσεως ὑμῶν τύχητε. καὶ τὸν
[παρ]αδιδοῦντα τὰ γρ[ά]μματα κατηχ[ο]ύμε-
νον πιστὸν προσδέξασθε. προσαγορεύ-
σ̣α̣τε παν̣τ̣α [. . . . .]τον
-- -- -- -- -- -- -- -- -- -- -- -- -- --

Verso: Θωμ̣[ᾶ]ς̣ *vacat* ιυ[. . .] . α Χ *vacat* Παύ̣[λῳ̣ ±?

6 ἀσφαλείσητε = ἀσφαλίσητε (ἀσφαλίσηται?)

Thomas and . . . and those with us . . . to Paul. . . greetings. Since . . . we said . . . to you to greet you . . . that you may be secure (*or* that he may assure you) concerning the . . . and concerning the care and . . . your divine exercise . . . But God . . . assisting you in all things . . . of (*or* from) affliction . . . and I exhort . . . in (?) meditation and in divinity until you finally obtain your rest. And receive the faithful catechumen passing on this letter. Salute all . . .

Recto: 1 The readings are very uncertain for much of this line, especially the οἱ σὺν ἡμῖν, which could be another name instead. However, compare the opening of *P.Got.* 11 (Naldini, *Cristianesimo* no. 23), οἱ σὺν ἐμοί. οἱ σὺν ἐμοί is also found in the closing greeting of all the letters of peace. A fold in the papyrus makes the stroke just before συν look very close, but it is certainly a separate letter and probably not ligatured with what precedes it. There is certainly enough ink and space to justify another word after ἡμῖν; I have supplied πάντες on the basis of parallels: Athanasius, προσαγορεύουσί σε πάντες οἱ σὺν ἡμῖν, *Epistula ad Maximum* 51.26.1089 and σὲ οἱ σὺν ἡμῖν πάντες προσαγορεύουσίν, *Epistula ad Epictetum* 110.12.23; Basil, Οἱ σὺν ἡμῖν πάντες ἀσπάζονται and οἱ σὺν ἡμῖν πάντες προσαγορεύουσίν, *Epistulae* 4.161.31-2 and 4.264.23-4.

2 ιωτ. Perhaps some form of τιμιώτατος? See Tibiletti, *Lettere* 35.

6 ἀσφαλείσητε 'Ασφαλίζω, secure, protect, assure, fortify (see PGL s.v.). Compare John Chrysostom, *De paenitentia et in lectionem de Davide* PG64.14.8-9 . . . ἀλλὰ τὴν ὑμετέραν ζωὴν ἀσφαλίζομαι, ἵνα ὅταν πολλὰ κατορθώσῃς, ἀσφαλίσῃς σαυτὸν, ἵνα μὴ πέσῃς. The active is well-attested, and if the spelling of the ending is correct, then the person is second plural, in keeping with the rest of the letter. However, the middle voice is more common, and a simple phonetic interchange would make it ἀσφαλίσηται, "that he may strengthen (you)." Compare the entire letter with, e.g., Pseudo-Macarius, *Sermones* 64 *(collectio B)* 34.13, ἐγγίζει τις τῇ πόλει ἐκείνῃ καὶ εἴς τινα βαθμὸν ἔτι ἐλλείπεται, ἐὰν μὴ ἀσφαλίσηται, ἀλλ᾽ἐκτραπῇ ἀπώλεσε τὰ πάντα καὶ ἠλλοτριώθη τῆς ἀναπαύσεως. εἰσὶ δὲ ἄλλοι βοηθούμενοι ὑπὸ τοῦ κυρίου *κτλ.*

7-8, 12 τὴν μελέτην, θείαν ἄσκησιν, τῆι μελέτηι. Μελέτη has a perfectly everyday meaning—care, exercise, practice, usage—but since it is used here in connection with ἀσφαλίζω, θεία ἄσκησις, and θειότης, it seems likely that it has a specifically Christian connotation (see PGL s.v.). The word is very frequent in the Fathers for study (especially of the Bible) or meditation. μετὰ τῶν εἰδότων, ὅτι ἡ μελέτη ἐστὶν ἔργον εὐφροσύνης, καὶ ἀναμαρυκωμένων τόν λόγον κυρίου, *Barnabae Epistula* 10.11.

It is hardly surprising that ἄσκησις is very frequent in the Fathers. I have found only one instance so far of its use with θεῖα: Πῶς οὖν διακρίνωμεν τὴν θείαν καὶ βασιλικὴν ἄσκησιν τῆς τυραννικῆς καὶ δαιμονιώδους; Amma Syncletica in the *Apothegmata Patrum*, PG65.425c; similarly, τὴν ἄσκησιν τῶν θείων μαθημάτων, Methodius *Symposium* 9.4.247 (PG18.186a). For an interesting pagan use, see *P.Oxy.* XLII 3069.9-10.

Ἄσκησις and μελέτη used together: Ἐκ μελέτης πολλῆς καὶ ἀσκήσεως ἡ βία καὶ ἀγριότης τῶν παθῶν ἀσθενεῖς, Didymus the Blind *Ad philosophum*, PG39.1109b; Δεῖ γὰρ καθαροὺς καὶ κεκοσμημένους ἥκειν εἰς τὴν ἑορτήν, ὥσπερ κοσμέτρῳ ταῖς ἀσκήσεσι καὶ μελέταις τῆς ἀρετῆς πεφιλοπονημένους· ὅτι μελέταις ἐπιπόνοις καὶ ἀσκήσεσι καθαιρόμενος ὁ νοῦς . . . ὀξυδορκεῖ πρὸς τὴν ἀλήθειαν, also τὴν ἄσκησιν καὶ μελέτην τῶν Γραφῶν, Methodius *Symposium* 9.4.247-8.

10-11 τῆς κακώσεως. PGL, "ill-treatment, esp. of divine affliction." τὰ δὲ παιδεύοντα καὶ διὰ τῆς κακώσεως εἰς ἐπιστροφὴν ἄγοντα, Basil *Regulae brevius tractatae*, question 276 (PG31.1273d); κάκωσιν δὲ τὴν νηστείαν ὠνόμασεν, Theodoret *Quaestiones in Leviticum* 16, question 22.

13 τῆι θειότητι. It is difficult to see what precisely θειότης, "deity," "divinity," is meant to signify here. Linked with the preceding μελέτης, and in the context of ἄσκησις and κάκωσις, however, it presumably refers to practice, usage, discipline, or instruction; the exercise, or acquisition, of divinity. Cf. 2 Pet.1:4, ἵνα διὰ τούτων γένησθε θείας κοινωνοὶ φύσεως, "that we may become partakers of the divine nature;" Eusebius Pamphilus, ἵνα μηκέτι ὦμεν πολλοὶ, ἀλλ' οἱ πάντες εἷς, ἑνωθέντες αὐτοῦ τῇ θειότητι . . . κατὰ δὲ τελείωσιν τῆς εἰς ἄκραν ἀρετῆς, also φῶτα καὶ αὐτοὶ . . . γενησόμενοι καὶ Υἱοὶ Θεοῦ κατὰ μετοχὴν τῆς τοῦ μονογενοῦς αὐτοῦ κοινωνίας ἀποτελεσθέντες μετουσίᾳ τῶν τῆς θεότητος αὐτοῦ μαρμαρυγῶν, *De Ecclesiastica Theologia* 3.18; and in general the patristic doctrine of θέωσις, 'deification.'

13 μέχρις οὗ. See Gignac, *Grammar* 1:126-128 on the use of a terminal sigma with μέχρι.

13-14 τῆς ἀναπαύσεως. Among the many meanings of ἀνάπαυσις given in PGL, relevant to what I earlier termed the vocabulary of sanctification: "result of training in practice of virtue," "consisting in spiritual perfection," ἡ τοῦ τελείου καὶ γνωστικοῦ . . . ἀνάπαυσις, Clement *Paedogogus* 1.6 (Marrou *et al.* edition, 1:174; PG8.292b); τῷ κυρίῳ δὲ κολλωμένη . . . ψυχὴ . . . ἀπὸ ἀναπαύσεως εἰς τελειοτέραν ἀναπαύσεως μετατίθεται, Macarius of Egypt *De Charitate* 28 (PG34.932b); ἀπὸ δόξης εἰς δόξαν καὶ ἀπὸ ἀναπαύσεως εἰς ἀναπαύσεις ἐνεργεστέρας καὶ τελειοτέρας μετατίθεσθαι καταξιοῦται, Macarius *Sermones* 52.2.8. See also the citation from Pseudo-Macarius in the note on line 6 above.

Verso: After Θωμ̣[ᾶ]ς it is difficult to tell how much is blank space and how much is lost due to fading and abrasion. There are a few traces of ink around the holes in the papyrus before and after the alpha in the middle of the line.

299. Christian Letter

Inv. 174b | 10.5 x 7 cm. | IV

Pl. 7 | | Provenance unknown

The papyrus is a fragment of a letter, with the first eight lines more or less complete. It is, however, torn in spots, particularly on the right side, where strands of papyrus with ink, pulled out of place, are folded or overlap.

Dating is especially important in determining the significance of the document. Unfortunately, this is difficult. The hand is easily read. The letters are fairly well formed and usually separated, although with some ligatures. The strokes are thick. There is no discernible tilt to the right. There are some cursive letter forms, e.g., the alpha. Still, the hand is a little clumsy; it cannot be called neat or attractive, though it is perfectly easy to read where the papyrus is not damaged. It is certainly not a Byzantine hand,[74] but it is hardly distinctive otherwise; hands of a similar type can be found as early as the second century, e.g., *P.Vindob.Sijp.* 8, plate IV, dated 127 AD. I would place **299** in the fourth century. Compare *P.Heid.* I 6, plate 60, dated by Kenyon to the mid-fourth century, a hand somewhat less neat than ours, and *P.Lond.* III 981, p. 294, reproduced in the facsimile volume III, plate 74, from the Abinnaeus archive, a neater, more practised hand than ours.

The style of the opening five lines is no more conclusive for dating, continuing throughout the late Roman and early Byzantine periods, although the opening address is often dropped by the sixth century.[75] Μοναχός (line 7) is found in the documentary tradition mainly in the fourth century, largely replaced by μονάζων in the fifth, but it remains in

---

74 E.g., as defined by E. A. Thompson, *An Introduction to Greek and Latin Palaeography* (Oxford 1912) 151, 174-184, or Montevecchi, *Papirologia* 54.

75 Compare *P.Oxy.* II 258, 2nd century; *P.Oxy.* XIV 1668, 3rd century; *P.Lond.* II 417 p. 299, from the Abinnaeus archive, mid-fourth century; *P.Bour.* 25, 4th century. Dropping the opening address: see, e.g., the letters in *P.Oxy.* XVI.

the literary tradition and turns up in the documentary again in the sixth.[76]

All this taken together suggests a fourth or early fifth century date, but the possibility of a later date cannot be ruled out.

The relationship between the sender and the recipient is impossible to ascertain and made all the more puzzling by the use of δεσπότης to address a woman, although this does not necessarily imply any great social distance between the two (see notes). The reference to a παραγαύτιον (see note), apparently an expensive garment, indicates a middle class, if not fairly well-to-do, milieu. This is not surprising and is consistent with the documentary evidence of the third and fourth centuries. By the early third century, Christians of Arsinoe in Egypt included men of sufficient station to be nominated to local office.[77] E. A. Judge and S. R. Pickering, in a survey of thirty-nine documentary papyri relevant to Christianity down to the mid-fourth century (personal correspondence, letters involving churches, official enquiries, public records, petitions, wills and other contractual documents) find that "prominent . . . are individuals who belong to the governing circles of the metropolitan cities. This presupposes wealth, the means to travel, and, in general, the kind of stake in life that calls for documentation." Still others, marked out by their evident education or financial connections, "are probably also not far removed from the upper levels of metropolitan life."[78]

The principal interest of the papyrus lies in the unnamed μοναχός of line 7. What is a monk doing with a παραγαύτιον? Why should he be delivering it to an apparently secular individual?

P.Col. VII 171,[79] is the earliest reference to a μοναχός (in the sense of "monk"), datable precisely to 324. It is even earlier than the first literary attestation of the monastic movement.[80] The text is a petition to the *praepositus* by Isidoros of Karanis,[81] who relates how he was rescued

---

[76] E. A. Judge, "Fourth-century monasticism in the papyri," in *Proceedings of the XVIth International Congress of Papyrology*, R. S. Bagnall et al., eds. (Chico, CA 1981) 617.

[77] See P. van Minnen, "The Roots of Egyptian Christianity," *APF* 40 (1994) 73-76.

[78] E. A. Judge and S. R. Pickering, "Papyrus documentation of church and community in Egypt to the mid-fourth century," *JbAC* 20 (1977) 42-71, esp. 69-70.

[79] Originally published as *P.Coll.Youtie* 77; republished with commentary by E. A. Judge in *New Docs1976*, 124-6.

[80] Eusebius, *Commentaria in Psalmos* 67.7 (PG23.688-92).

[81] A well known figure. See the introductions to *P.Cair. Isid.* and *P.Col.* VII.

by Antoninos, διάκων, and Isak, μοναχός, after being set upon by men with whom he had a dispute. Both Antoninos and Isak are identified matter-of-factly, their occupations apparently unexceptionable, requiring no further identification or explanation. There is nothing to suggest that Isak is following either an eremitic or cenobitic form of monasticism. He appears to be of local origin.

E. A. Judge has considered this text in relation to the ἀποτακτικοί, long known from the literary tradition and more recently from the documentary papyri (including *P.Oxy.* XLIV 3203, μοναχαὶ ἀποτακτικαί) as a form of celibate Christian life, though neither eremitic nor cenobitic.[82] Rather, they remained within the local community, organized in households, connected with the local church, self-sufficient and even property-owning. Judge hypothesises that μοναχός was early used by the public to refer to the ἀποτακτικοί, a recognized τάγμα within the church comparable to the virgins and widows, and originating in the late third/early fourth century, as well as to those who took to the eremitic or cenobitic forms of monasticism. Still more documentary evidence of a monasticism that does not fall into either eremitic or cenobitic categories comes from the fourth century archive of the monk Nepheros (*P.Neph.*). The correspondence of Nepheros likewise reveals a monastic community whose members owned private property, made loans, and engaged in significant business transactions.[83]

There were certainly plenty of μοναχοί in the village and city life of Egypt by the end of the fourth century. The *Historia Monachorum* (chapter 5) says that there were monks in every quarter of Oxyrhynchus, as many as 5,000 in all. Jerome, speaking of the three types of monasticism in Egypt—anchorites, cenobites, and what he refers to as *remnuoth,* evidently the ἀποτακτικοί[84]—thought little of these city monks:

---

82 E. A. Judge, "The earliest use of monachos for 'monk' (P.Coll.Youtie 77) and the origins of monasticism," *JbAC* 20 (1977) 72-89; Judge, *XVI Congress,* 613-20; see also *DACL* s.v. "Apotactites et Apotaxamènes" 1:2604-26; A. Emmet, "Female ascetics in the Greek papyri," *JŒByz* 32.2 (1982) 507-515. G. M. Parássoglou, "Request for Help," *Miscellania Papirologica Ramon Roca-Puig* (Barcelona 1987) 247-250, redates *P.Lond.* III 1014, which mentions an ἀποτακτικός, to the fourth century. See also Bagnall, *Egypt* 297.

83 See the introduction to *P.Neph.* pages 17-20.

84 Judge, "Earliest use of monachos for 'monk' (P.Coll.Youtie 77) and the origins of monasticism," *JbAC* 20 (1977) 78-80; the editors of *P.Neph.* also identfiy the community of Nepheros with the *remnuoth.* On the coptic derivation of *remnuoth* and the description of a "third way" of monasticism in Jerome and John Cassian, see

Hi bini vel terni nec multo plures simul habitant suo arbitratu ac dicione viventes et de eo, quod laboraverint, in medium partes conferunt, ut habeant alimenta communia. Habitant autem quam plurimum in urbibus et castellis, et, quasi ars sit sancta, non vita, quidquid vendiderint, maioris est pretii. (*Epistulae* 22.34)

These dwell together by twos or threes, not many more, living according to their own will and authority, and from each comes a part of their earnings, that they may have a common store of food. They live however for the most part in cities and fortified towns, and, as though their craftsmanship should be holy, not their life, whatever they sell, the price is high.

Though we have little to go on, our μοναχός is probably best placed here, with the ἀποτακτικοί, or local-community monks, rather than among anchorites or more Pachomian monks. Could the παραγαύτιον be one of the items which are *maioris pretii*?

Recto: τῇ δεσπ[ό]τ̣ῃ μου καὶ [τ]ιμ̣ι̣ω̣[τάτῃ ἀ]δ̣[ελφ]ῇ
τημηπ . . . ρ̣ικισμανλ . .
πρὼ μὲν πάντων εὔχωμαι τῷ πα̣ν̣-
ελεήμονι Θεῷ π̣ε̣ρὶ τῆς ὑγίας σ[ο]ῦ̣· τοῦ-
τω γὰρ ἀντὶ παντός μοι ἐσστίν. καθὸς
δὲ γεγράφηκας μοι περὶ τοῦ π̣α̣ραγαυ̣-
τίου, ἤνεκεν μοι τοῦτω ὁ μοναχὸς καὶ
τοῦτο σοι ἀπέσστιλα περὶ̣ . . . . [
πολλὰ η[.]..[.].[....].[..]..[±9]

Verso: τῇ κυρίᾳ μου ἀδ[ελφῇ ±?

3 πρὼ = πρὸ εὔχωμαι = εὔχομαι 4 ὑγίας = ὑγιείας
4, 5, 7 τοῦτω = τοῦτο 5 ἐσστίν = ἐστίν καθός = καθώς
7 ἤνεκεν = ἤνεγκεν 8 ἀπέσστιλα = ἀπέστειλα

J. Horn, "Tria sunt in Aegypto genera monachorum" in *Quaerentes Scientiam: Festgabe für Wolfhart Westendorf* (Göttingen 1994) 63-82.

(Recto) To my mistress and most honored sister (?) . . . Before all else I pray to the all-merciful God for your health, for this concerns me more than anything. Just as you wrote to me about the *paragaution,* the monk has brought this to me and I have sent it to you for . . .

(Verso) To my lady and sister . . .

1-4 and verso. The reconstruction in line 1 after καί is quite conjectural. The iota-mu seems fairly clear, but there are only hints for what could be a following iota-omega. There is only a bottom stroke for the delta and a fragment of what could be the right vertical stroke of an eta.

In line 2, several letters can be easily read, but the gaps are such that I can make no sense out of the line. It probably contains the sender's name. We would expect it to contain χαίρειν or some other such, but a close examination shows this to be impossible.

Such an opening address, together with the health wish, is typical; cf. *P.Batav.* 21.1-4 (sixth century): Τῇ κυρίᾳ μου τιμ[ιωτάτῃ ἀδε]λφῇ Ν̣ό̣ν̣[νῃ]/ ὁ ἀδελφὸς Ἰσά̣[κιο]ς/ Πρὸ μὲν πάντων εὔχ[ο]μαι τῷ/ π̣α̣ντοκράτορι̣ Θεῷ ὡς ὑγιένο̣υσῃ *κτλ.; P.Lips.* 111.1-4 (Naldini, *Cristianesimo* no. 57; fourth century): Τῷ δεσπό[τῃ μ]ου καὶ ἀδελφῷ/ Ἰσι[δώ]ρῳ Σίων χαίρειν./ Πρὸ μὲν [πά]ντων εὔχομαι τῷ ὑψίστῳ θε[ῷ] περὶ/ τῆς σῆς ὑγίας καὶ ὁλοκληρίας *κτλ.;* also *P.Oxy.* XIV 1683.1-5 (Naldini, *Cristianesimo* no. 65; fourth century); *BGU* III 948.4-5 (Naldini, *Cristianesimo* no. 93; fourth/fifth century). However, although the addressee is clearly a woman—the address on the verso is unmistakable—and despite the damage to the papyrus, the best reading for the beginning of line 1 is still τῇ δεσπότῃ and not, as we might expect, τῇ δεσποίνῃ or δεσποίνᾳ. Cf. *PSI* IV 301, Τῇ δεσποίνῃ μου ὡς ἀληθῶς κατ̣ὰ/ [π]άντα θαυμασιωτάτῃ ἀδελφῇ/ Ἀθανασίᾳ *κτλ.*, dated by the editor to the fifth century.

1 τῇ δεσπότῃ. As κύριος gradually became little more than a polite epithet or expression of affection in private correspondence, δεσπότης acquired an honorific value. In patristic letters it is commonly used for bishops and laymen of rank, at times together with τιμιωτάτος, Dinneen, *Titles* 56-7, while δέσποινα is reserved for women of high

standing, Dinneen, *Titles* 76. By the fourth century, however, both δεσπότης and δέσποινα were already losing some of that significance, even when combined with τιμιωτάτος, to judge from the papyri; cf. *CPR* V 23, *P.Harr.* I 112, *P.Ant.* II 93. See Tibiletti, *Lettere* 32-33.

τιμιωτάτῃ. The term is used for all classes, though it may suggest that the sender considers the recipient a social superior. See Tibiletti, *Lettere* 35. Chrysostom used it to address both men and women in his letters, Dinneen, *Titles* 73-5.

ἀδελφῇ. 'Αδελφός/ ἀδελφή can signify a general sentiment, not specifically Christian, cf. *P.Herm.* 6. It can also mean sibling, monk, or even husband and wife—see Naldini, *Cristianesimo* pages 15-6, and Naldini, *Cristianesimo* no. 196. The expression τῇ δεσπ[ό]τ̣ῃ μου suggests a figurative, rather than literal, meaning, cf. *P.Herm.* 6.

3-4 πανελεήμων. PGL gives only two citations: T. Ruinart, ed., *Acta Martyrum* (Ratisbon 1859) 452, and John Chrysostom, *In secundam ad Corinthios epistolam commentarius: Homilia II* (PG61.399). Tibiletti, *Lettere* 114 states that formulaic attributions to God of mercy or pity, such as οἰκτίρμων, ἐλεήμων, or πανελεήμων, appear "raramente" in the papyri. Yet πανελεήμων turns up in a fourth/fifth century letter (*P.Ross.Georg.* III 10.4 = Naldini, *Cristianesimo* no. 90; see Naldini's note) in exactly the same position as here: Π[ρὸ] μὲν [πα]ντὸς ε[ὔ]χομε τῷ πανελεήμονι Θεῷ ὅπως [ὑ]γιένοτός σου . . . and similarly in *P.Oxy.* XLVIII 3421, *P.Oxy.* LVI 3864 and 3865, *P.Iand.* VI 103, *P.Wash.Univ.* II 108, and also appears in an emancipation document of 355 AD (Mitteis, *Chrestomathie* 361.8, 355 AD, the only citation in LSJ—see R. S. Bagnall, K. A. Worp, "Chronological Notes on Byzantine Documents, I," *BASP* 15 (1978) 235-6 for the date, bibliography and discussion of this text); in a fourth/fifth century liturgical fragment (Kurt Treu, "Varia Christiana II," *APF* 32 (1986) no. 4.6); and *SB* X 10522. The passage from Chrysostom is interesting, for it is not Chrysostom himself speaking, but rather quoting from what he takes to be a well-known portion of the liturgy, the prayer for the catechumens. If the word is rare in the literary tradition, it was evidently still well-known then, as the papyri attest.

6 παραγαύτιον. The papyrus is damaged and a bit twisted here, but examination under magnification shows this to be the most likely reading. If correct, it is a unique spelling of an interesting word. It is evidently some sort of shirt or tunic. The term is used as both noun and adjective, e.g., λινούδιον παραγαύδιον in *P.Oxy.* VII 1026.12 (fifth century; see *APF* 5 (1913) 408 or *BL* I 330 for the corrected reading), and στιχαρομαφόριον παραγαυδωτόν in *P.Oxy.* XVI 1978.3, a list of articles of

dress (sixth century). LSJ defines παραγαύδης as a "garment with a purple border," based on a passage from Lydus (sixth century), who described it as an ancient patrician garment, "tunics, ornamented with spearheads, purple-edged, entirely white" and wrote that Octavian, in his role as pontifex, wore "aurigammous paragodai, namely 'tunics trimmed with little gold gammas,'" *de Magistratibus populi Romani* 1.17, 2.4, trans. A. C. Bandy (Philadelphia 1983). LSJ also lists παραγαύδιον, παραγαῦδιν, παρακαυτωδόν, and παρακαυδωτόν as variants, but gives no etymology. Preisigke, *Wörterbuch* points to a Latin root and defines the adjective παρακαυδωτόν as "mit Schwänzen [< *cauda*] versehen," while the editor of *P.Heid.* VII 406, a λόγος ἱματίων, suggests "Troddeln," bobs or tassels, instead of "Schwänzen," tails. See LSJ, Preisigke's *Wörterbuch*, and *P.Heid.* VII 406 for other examples. The term appears in later Latin as *paragauda*; and entries for this and for the adjectives *paragaudatus* and *paragaudius* in A. Souter, *A Glossary of Later Latin to 600 A.D.* (Oxford 1949) suggest that the παραγαύτιον of **299** is probably some sort of tunic with trimming.

300. Christian Letter

Inv. 417 | 9 x 16 cm. | IV

Pl. 8 | Provenance unknown

The papyrus is badly damaged. The recto is particularly marred, with several holes, tears, and much fading of ink, as well as an uncertain amount of text missing from the right and bottom, making interpretation difficult. The text of the verso is more or less complete for the first nine lines. The ink is faded there too, but in general it is much easier to make out than the recto. The text is written across the fibers on both recto and verso; thus "recto" here designates only the side with an address at the beginning of the text. On the verso there are unreadable traces of ink to the right of the text on the more badly damaged portion of the papryus, perhaps the remains of a second column of text.

The document is clearly a letter, following the usual conventions. Line 3 is part of the prayer for the recipients' health, line 4 the "informational formula."[85] The hand is semi-cursive, careful, based on uncial forms, with a slight slope to the left (more apparent on the verso). It is easy to read where the condition permits. There are few ligatures except (regularly) alpha-iota. I would judge it to be fourth century. It resembles to a degree the hand of *P.Abinn.* 6 and 8, dated to 346, although the latter is somewhat more confident and cursive.[86] There is one clear case of diaeresis on line 9 of the verso, and perhaps another on line 2 of the recto. The spelling is phonetic, frequently substituting alpha-iota for epsilon and omicron for omega. There is an unusual exchange of sigma for delta three times on the verso (see notes).

The hand appears to be the same on both sides, despite slight differences. However, what connection there is between the text of the

---

85 F. X. J. Exler, *The Form of the Ancient Greek Letter* (Washington 1923) 107-111; White, *Ancient Letters* 200-1, 207; Koskenniemi, *Studien* 77-8, 139-45.

86 See plates 104 and 105 of the second atlas of *P.Lond.*

recto and that of the verso remains obscure. It is possible, though unlikely, that they are two different documents. The writer speaks in the plural on the recto and the singular on the verso; there is ample precedent for this, but he also uses the plural on the recto and the singular on the verso for the addressee. The two sides are written at right angles to each other. The verso, however, has no address (to A from B or some variation). Such opening phrases often got dropped in the correspondence of the fifth and sixth century,[87] but the recto begins in the customary manner, suggesting that the verso is a continuance. It could be the same writer on two different occasions, if one side is a draft for the same or an earlier letter, or a postscript added before mailing but at a later date.

If the two sides are connected, this may be a clue regarding the amount of text missing on the right side of the recto. The longest line on the verso is 25 letters; all the remaining lines have from 19 to 22 letters. This is despite the ample room on the right of the verso for continuing each line well beyond 19 to 25 letters. It is reasonable to assume that the writer observed a similar restraint on the recto from either choice or necessity. If the restorations for lines 2 and 9 of the recto are correct, they suggest lines of around 25 letters for the recto.

Recto:
Κύρι⟨ . ⟩ μου ἀδελφ . . . . . . [
κυρ̣ι̣ο̣ . ου υἱός . λ . . νος χ̣[αίρειν.]
. . πε . εὐχόμαθα περὶ τῆ[ς ὑμῶν]
φ[ι]λίας. εἰδέναι ὑμᾶς θ̣έ̣[λω ὅτι μέ-]
χρ̣ι τ̣ούτο⟨υ⟩ ὁλοκληροῦμ[εν
μι . . ηστουμαι ἐλθεῖ̣ν̣ . . . [
ελεσα σοῦ ἐξέπλεξα̣ . . [
λον αναστηκαι καὶ ταπ̣ε̣[
νιδος ἀλλὰ εὐχαρισστ̣[οῦμεν τῷ]
Θεῷ πάντα τὰ̣ . . φ̣ . . αν . [
αὐτὸς γὰ̣ρ ἐστὶν ὁ ἀπαιτ̣[
σον πρὸς ἐμὲ . . π̣ωται . [
ὅτι δὸς ἐ̣μ[οι . . . .] ια . οπ[
εξα̣γη βω . . [. . . . .]ενα[

---

87 See for example the letters in *P.Oxy.* XVI.

καὶ τ̣ο̣ὺς πα̣λτ ̣[̣ ̣ ̣ ̣ ̣]υ̣ς κα̣[
 ̣] ̣ ̣[̣ ̣ ̣] ̣πετυ[̣ ̣ ̣ ̣ ̣]αιπ ̣[
 ̣ ̣ ̣ ̣ ̣ ̣ ̣]οις π[̣ ̣ ̣ ̣ ̣] ̣ ̣ ̣[
 ̣ ̣ ̣ ̣ ̣ ̣ ̣]χ̣αι ̣[
 ̣ ̣ ̣ ̣ ̣ ̣ ̣]χ̣α̣ιρ̣[
 ̣ ̣ ̣ ̣ ̣ ̣ ̣] ̣ μ ̣ ̣[
 ̣ ̣ ̣ ̣ ̣ ̣ ̣] ̣ μ̣ ̣[

Verso: ἔ̣π̣ε̣μψα σοὶ σιὰ Εὐτυχία̣ς̣
κν̣ί̣σιο̣ν γάρου ἔχον φρα-
τ̣ιδα ἐνναία καὶ τὸ μαφό̣ρ̣-
τιον τὸ λευκὸν καὶ κο̣ΐκιο[ν]
ψομίον ἔχον ζεύγη εἴκοσι.
ὥσπερ οὖν οὐσὲ ζημιῶμα̣ι̣
ἀλλὰ ναινίκκηκαι, νινκῆ-
σ̣ο̣ν καὶ σὺ μετὰ τῆς γεούχου σοῦ̣
ὕ̣π̣ερ ιζ ̣ νυ ̣ ος οὐδὲ ̣ ̣ ̣ ̣ ος
[±9]ος εὐκ[±12]

Recto 3 εὐχόμαθα = εὐχόμεθα 8 αναστηκαι = ἀνέστηκε?
9 εὐχαρισστοῦμεν = εὐχαριστοῦμεν 12 ̣πωται = ὁπότε?
Verso 1 σιὰ = διὰ 2 κνίσιον = κνίδιον 3 ἐνναία = ἐννέα
5 ψομίον = ψωμίων 6 οὐσὲ = οὐδὲ 7 ναινικκηκαι = νενίκηκα
7-8 νινκῆσον = νικῆσον 9 papyrus ϊζ

(Verso) I sent to you through Eutuchia a knidion of fish-sauce with nine *phratida* and the white veil and a little basket of loaves containing twenty pairs. Therefore just as I am not suffering financial loss but have won, now you prevail with your landlord over . . .

Recto: 1-2 The letter appears to begin with the formula "to B, A," common by the fourth century and usually followed by χαίρειν or some variation (Exler 33-4; White, *Ancient Letters* 195). However, there are apparently two addressees, separately designated κύριος rather than together in the plural in the beginning. There is damage to the papyrus after κυρ- and before -ου on both lines, and in each case there is what looks like the tail of a mu before the -ου. If we read μου, however, there is no space for any letter after κυρι- in line 1 and very little space after κυρι- in line 2 for a large letter such as omega. Traces of ink on line 2 suggest κυριο, perhaps a misspelling of κυρίῳ. The writer frequently uses omicron in place of omega; still, the Θεῷ of line 10 of the recto indicates that he knows the proper ending for a masculine dative (but compare the openings of *CPJ* 479 and *P.Ross.Georg.* III 10). The double address could be due to a difference in sex, κύρι⟨ᾳ⟩ for line 1 and κυριο (= κυρίῳ) for line 2.

We should expect a name or relation in the dative to follow the first two words of line 2. What follows is υιοσ ̣λ ̣ ̣ νοσ. There appears to be a line over υιο and another line connecting the top of the lambda with the letter (possibly an iota or perhaps two letters) preceding. It might be that the mark beginning over the upsilon is only stray ink and the line over and touching the iota is another diaeresis such as that on the verso. The entire two lines could be reconstructed as:

1 Κύρι⟨ᾳ⟩ μου ἀδελφῇ (name in dative) καὶ (name in dative)

2 κυρίο μου υἱο, Σιλβανὸς χαίρειν

or

2 κυρίο μου, υἱός (name in nominative), χαίρειν (see *P.Oxy.* I 123).

Something like this is probably the answer. However, it would be unusual for the name of an addressee to precede κυρίῳ. Also, the line over υιο does not look like a diaeresis; the diaeresis on the verso is clearly two dots. Moreover, this leaves the line over ̣λ unaccounted for, though this seems an unlikely occasion for a *nomen sacrum*.

2 χαίρειν. The χ is conjectural since the letter fragment is so small. The restoration is based on innumerable parallels.

2-3 What comes before εὐχόμαθα? Πρὸ μὲν πάντων is the usual expression but does not fit in well either with the traces of letters before εὐχόμαθα or with a reasonable length for the previous line. Naldini, *Cristianesimo* 196-7, 200-1; Koskenniemi, *Studien* 139-145.

3-4 We should expect ὁλοκληρίας, σωτηρίας, ὑγιείας or εὐρωστίας after the περὶ τῆς of line 3, but none of these fits in easily with the fragments of letters before εἰδέναι.

4-5 εἰδέναι ὑμᾶς θέ[λω ὅτι μέ-]χρι̣ τ̣ούτο⟨υ⟩ ὁλοκληροῦμ[εν. "I want you to know that up until now we are in good health." Compare *SB* XII 10772.3-4: γινώσκειν ὑμ[ᾶς θέλω] ὅτι/ μέχρι τούτου ὁλοκληρό[ς εἰμι, *P.Mich.* III 219 (*SB* 7251, Naldini, *Cristianesimo* no. 16).4-5: [γινώ]σκιν ὑμᾶς θέλω ὅτι θεοῦ θέλον-/ [τος ὁλοκληροῦμεν, also *P.Oxy.* XIV 1770.6-8: γ[ινώσκειν]/ ὑμᾶς θέλω ὅτι μετ[ὰ πάντων]/ ὁλοκληροῦμεν.

8-9 ταπ̣ε̣[/ νιδος. The text of the recto is too fragmentary to restore anything here with confidence, but it is tempting to provide something like τὰ πε(accusative object) (name in dative)νι δός.

9 εὐχαρισστ̣[οῦμεν. Restored on the basis of the first person plural in line 5.

10 Θεῷ is written with the superscript line associated with *nomina sacra* but without the usual contraction. Uncontracted *nomina sacra* are rare but not unknown. The best example is *P.Lond.* VI 1917, a long fourth century letter from a Meletian monk who consistently overlines words like Θεός, 'Ιησοῦς, and πνεῦμα, while never contracting them. Even more like **300** is *P.Abinn.* 6, a letter from the priest and/or monk Apa Mios, where Θεῷ, Θεόν, and ὁ κύριος ὁ Θεός are all overlined and uncontracted (while κυρίῳ is both overlined and contracted twice). *P.Abinn.* 6 was evidently dictated by Apa Mios, and same hand may have written two other letters for him, *P.Abinn.* 8 and 19 (H. I. Bell et al., eds., *The Abinnaeus Archive: Papers of a Roman Officer in the Reign of Constantius II* (Oxford 1962) 44), which employ *nomina sacra* in the same manner (*P.Abinn.* 7, also from Apa Mios but dictated to a different amanuensis, has contractions for κ(υρί)ῳ with no overline). Both L. Traube (*Nomina Sacra: Versuch einer Geschichte der Christlichen Kürzung* (Munich 1907) 49-50) on the Abinnaeus archive and Bell on *P.Lond.* VI 1917 concluded, in Bell's words, that "contracted forms of *nomina sacra,* though well established, were not yet completely understood by the less literate writers." (*P.Lond.* VI pages 80-1)

The hands that produced *P.Lond.* 1917, *P.Abinn.* 6 (both from an ecclesiastical background and of about the same date) and **300**, though characterized by poor spelling, syntax, etc., show knowledge of something, viz. *nomina sacra,* that probably came from studying a text, most likely the Bible. This fixation on a text, even to using an imperfectly understood principle from it in correspondence, raises again the question of an impetus to literacy provided by Christianity; see the discussion above for **294**.

Verso: 1-2 σιά, κνίσιον. It is impossible to read διά or κνίδιον. The formation of the deltas elsewhere is quite regular and does not resemble these letters at all, which are identical to the sigmas of this document. Gignac does not mention the interchange of sigma and delta. He does, however, show the stages that could lead to it. Delta and zeta were frequently interchanged from the third century on, particularly before iota (Gignac, *Grammar* 1: 75-6). At the same time, zeta was frequently interchanged with sigma, reflecting Coptic pronunciation (Gignac, *Grammar* 1:120-4). The writer of **300** has taken this process a step further. *P.Naqlun* I 6.6, 'Ιδρ(αηλίτου) for 'Ισρ(αηλίτου), shows the same progression in reverse, due perhaps to the non-Greek origin of the word; see the editor's commentary.

2 A κνίδιον was almost always a measure for wine. It was also used for honey, e.g., *P.Ant.* III 194, smoked fish, e.g., *P.Ant.* II 96, and even money, *P.Coll.Youtie* II 84, *P.Giss.Univ.* III 22. For another example of measuring γάρον, "fish-sauce," see *P.Oxy.* XIV 1770 and *P.Oxy.* XLI 2893.

2-3 I cannot decipher the word that ends line 2 and begins line 3, and that looks like φρατιδα.

3-4 Μαφόρτιον, a common diminutive for μαφόρτης, a veil or headdress for women, priests and monks. Other variants include μαφόριον and μαφόριν. It appears as *maforte* in later Latin. It became a standard feature of monastic clothing (D. Montserrat, "A List of Monastic Garments from Oxyrhynchus," *BASP* 29 (1992) 83), but it is too common to make any such connection here. For a discussion and recent literature, see *P.Heid.* VII 406.r5 and commentary; for older literature, see A. Bazzero, "Maphortes," *Studi della Scuola Papirologica* 2 (1917) 95-102.

κοΐκιο[ν], "little basket," a diminutive of κόϊξ; see *P.Oslo* III 159 r.13, *ZPE* 35 (1979) 126.

6 οὐσὲ See note on verso 1-2 above. However, the delta of οὐδὲ on line 9 seems clear.

ἀπαιτ[Perhaps ἀπαιτ[ῶν or ἀπαιτ[ητής. If the latter, then this and the reference to the landlord on line 8 of the verso suggest that part of the subject of the letter is taxation, which in turn suggests that the ζημιῶμαι should be translated "fined." See *P.Monac.* I 14.19.

7 The author is clearly referring to himself by using the first person singular ζημιῶμαι in line 6, which makes the interpretation of ναινίκκηκαι in 7 difficult. If ναινίκκηκαι is read as the third person perfect νενίκηκε, then the subject has shifted in mid-sentence: "I am not suffering financial loss but he has won." However, given the implied contrast with the imperative νικῆσον that follows, it seems more likely that the writer has slipped by using the same alpha-iota ending employed in the previous ζημιῶμαι and we should understand νενίκηκα, "I have prevailed."

7-8 νινκῆσον = νικῆσον. On the insertion of a medial nasal, see Gignac, *Grammar* 2: 118-9.

301. Christian Letter

Inv. 126 | 9 x 12 cm. | IV

Pl. 9 | | Provenance unknown

The text is a fragment of a letter; it is missing the opening line(s) of the address and breaks off after thirteen lines. An uncertain amount of text is missing from the right side, though the suggested readings would make the average line about twenty-six to twenty-eight letters long. It is worn and faded, with many holes.

The hand is somewhat cursive, but not difficult to read where the condition of the papyrus does not interfere. There are some ligatures, but most letters are separate. There is no particular tilt, and none of the characteristics of a Byzantine hand.[88] I cannot find a really close match, but the hand seems best placed in the fourth or fourth/fifth century; compare *P.Heid.* I 6, plate 60 (text Naldini, *Cristianesimo* no. 41) and the plate in *Cd'E* 42 (1967) 137-9 (text Naldini, *Cristianesimo* no. 69), as well as *P.Princ.* II 102. The name of the author, however, would strongly suggest a date in the fourth century (see below).

The author is a bishop named Psenamounios (a variant of Psenamounis), which means "son of Amon" in Egyptian. Christians, both clergy and lay, with unambiguously pagan names are the rule rather than the exception for the first three centuries of our era; the change to unambiguously Christian names does not begin in earnest until the fourth century. Thereafter, the rate of change is rapid.[89] A

---

88 See note 71 above.

89 A. von Harnack, *The Mission and Expansion of Christianity in the First Three Centuries*, trans. J. Moffatt, 2nd ed., vol. 1 (London 1908) 422-430; R. S. Bagnall, "Religious Conversion and Onomastic Change in Early Byzantine Egypt," *BASP* 19 (1982) 105-123; E. Wipszycka, "La valeur de l'onomastique pour l'histoire de la christianisation de l'Égypte. A propos d'une étude de R. S. Bagnall," *ZPE* 62 (1986) 173-81; R. S. Bagnall, "Conversion and Onomastics: A Reply," *ZPE* 69 (1987) 243-50.

recent study finds no examples of Psenamounis after 350.[90] Unfortunately, there is no trace of a bishop Psenamounios either in the literary tradition or among the papyri.[91]

Only a fragment of the text remains, and of that much can be identified as formulas or clichés, common either in letters in general or Christian letters in particular. However, there are several echoes of fourth century letters requesting monastic prayer which suggest that this text is somehow related. In some of these letters, the request is added as an afterthought to the main subject, but most are simply requests for prayer, and give evidence of the early belief in the power of monastic intercession.[92]

The simplest of these letters contains only a brief, albeit urgent, request. In *P.Lond.* VI 1928, Heraclides asks the monk Paphnutius to pray for his illness, καὶ τῆς παρὰ τοῦ κρείττο[ν]ος/ διὰ τῶν εὐχῶν σου βο[η]θείας δ[εό]μεθα. Others, however, contain one or more of the following elements or clichés, not uncommon in themselves, but which in combination approach a specifically Christian formula: 1) a request to be remembered, using either μιμνήσκω or μνημονεύω, in the recipient's prayers; 2) a desire to be found worthy, whether by God or the recipient, using some form of καταξιόω, either of the recipient's prayers or of the recipient's receiving of τὰ γράμματα; 3) a reference to the recipient by pious epithet plus a possessive adjective or pronoun, e.g., τὴν σὴν θεοσέβειαν; 4) a hope that the sender will be remembered ceaselessly.

---

90 W. Clarysse, "The Coptic Martyr Cult" in *Martyium in Multidisciplinary Perspective,* ed. M. Lamberigts and P. van Deun, Bibliotheca Ephemeridum Theologicarum Lovaniensium CXVII (Leuven 1995), 384-389. My own check of some fifty cases of Psenamounios from our era listed in F. Preisigke, *Namenbuch* (Heidelberg 1922) and D. Foraboschi, *Onomasticon alterum papyrologicum* (Milan 1967-71) found only four as late as the fourth century and one in the sixth.

91 K. A. Worp, "A Checklist of Bishops in Byzantine Egypt," *ZPE* 100 (1994) 283-318. It was not unknown for a bishop to have such a name, Worp 318. Athanasius mentions a bishop Psenosiris (PG25.340a4, 653a5, 780a9), and there is a priest of the same name from the beginning of the fourth century—see *P.Grenf.* II 73 (Naldini, *Cristianesimo* no. 21). Naldini, *Cristianesimo* has a bibliography for this text, much commented upon.

92 Requests for prayer are found in the New Testament letters, e.g. 1 Thess. 5:25 and Romans 15:30; cf. also Philemon 4. We might expect them to be common; however, among 4th century and earlier Christian papyri, there is no instance of a request for prayer in Naldini, *P. Lond.* VI, or *P. Abinn.* that is not to or from a monk. On the style of such requests, see Tibiletti, *Lettere* 120-123.

P.Lond. VI 1923.12-14, to the monk Paphnutius: νῦν παρακαλῶ ὅπως/ μνημονεύσῃς μου ἐν τες/ ἁγίαις εὐχες σου.

P.Lond. VI 1925.3-5, 9-11, to Paphnutius: Εὐκαιρηθεὶς τοῦ [συ]ντε[ί]ν<ον>τος πρὸς τὴν θεοσέβειάν σου ἀνα[γκαῖ]ον ἡ[γ]ησάμην προσαγο-/ρεῦσαι τὴν εὐλά[βειά]ν σο[υ] διὰ γραμμάτων *κτλ*. . . . παρακαλῶ δὲ τὴν/ ἁγ[ιότητά σου ἵνα κ]ατ[α]ξιώσῃς εὔξασθαι *κτλ*.

P.Lond. VI 1926.15-17, to Paphnutius: Δέομε τῷ θεῷ δέομε/ κέ σοι μνήσθητί μου ἐν τῇ ἁγίᾳ σου/ προσευχῇ.

P.Lond. VI 1929.3-5, to Paphnutius: Ὁ π[α]ντοκ[ράτωρ] θεὸς καὶ ὁ Χρι[στὸς] αὐτοῦ δοίη τὴν σὴν θεοσέβειαν/ π[α]ραμένειν ἡ[μῖν] πολὺν [χ]ρό[νον] καὶ μεμνῆσ[θ]αι ἡμῶν ἐν ταῖς/ σαῖς προσε[υχαῖς].

Cd'E 13 (1938) 378 (Naldini, *Cristianesimo* no. 95).23-26, to the monk Horos: καταξίωσον/ δὲ μνησθῆναι ἡμ[ῶν] ἐκ τῶν ἁγίων ὑμῶν/ εὐχῶν.

P.Herm. 9 (Naldini, *Cristianesimo* no. 84).5-9, 13-16, to the monk Ioannes, addressed as an ἀποτακτικός: προσαγορεύω τὴν ἀμί-/μητόν σου διάθεσειν,/ δ[έ]σποτα, καὶ παρακαλῶ/ σ[ε] ὡς ἐν τῇ προσευχῇ/ μνηθῇς ἐμοῦ *κτλ*. . . . εὐλόγησόν/ με καὶ εὖξαι τῷ κυρίῳ/ μου θεῷ νυκτὸς καὶ ἡ-/μέραις περὶ ἐμοῦ.

P.Herm. 8 (Naldini, *Cristianesimo* no. 83).8-13, to the monk Ioannes: προσαγορεύω σου τοιγαροῦν τὴν εὐλάβειαν/ {σου} διὰ τούτων μου τ[ῶν γ]ραμμάτων, παρα-/καλῶν ὅπως μνημονεύσῃς κἀμοῦ τοῦ σε/ προσκυνοῦντος καὶ παντὸς τοῦ οἴκου μου/ ἐν αἷς ἀναπέμπεις [ἀεὶ] καὶ μεθ' ἡμέραν/ εὐχαῖς τῷ κυρίῳ σωτῆρει ἡμῶν.

P.Neph. 1.3-9 to the monk Ophellios: προηγουμένως εὐχόμεθα νυκτὸς/ καὶ ἡμέρας ὑγιαίνουσι ὑμῖν ψυχῇ καὶ/ σώματι τὰ παρ' ἡμῶν γράμματα ἀποδοθῆναι,/ ἔπειτα καὶ νῦν ὑπομνῆσαι ὑμῶν τὴν φιλαν-/θρωπίαν ὅπως ἐν ταῖς εὐχαῖς ὑμῶν/ μνημονεύσηται ὀνομάσαι ἡμᾶς διὰ τὴν/ ξενειτίαν ἡμῶν καὶ τῶν παιδίων ἡμῶν.

Also, at the end of a letter to a monastic community on the occasion of the death of their leader from Gregory Nazianzus (letter 238.7,

PG37.380): Ἐρρωμένους ὑμᾶς, ψυχῇ καὶ σώματι προκόπτοντας, ἐν τῇ δυνάμει τοῦ ἁγίου πνεύματος ὁ Κύριος σκεπάζοι μεμνημένους ἡμῶν ἐν ταῖς προσευχαῖς.[93]

A comparison of these texts with ours, particularly the underlined portions, shows that it is probable that this formula is somehow related to **301**, even though **301** itself is not a request for monastic prayer. Lines 9-10 appear to mean that the *sender*, Bishop Psenamounios, does not cease to remember the *recipient*, not the other way around. Instead, the formula suggests that the Bishop himself comes from a monastic milieu. Such language is found in at least one fourth century letter, not a request for prayer, *from* a monk to a non-monastic. *P.Amh.* II 145 (Naldini, *Cristianesimo* no. 49), after the initial address, opens with [Βούλο]μαι μὲν καταξιωθῆναι ἀεὶ γράφειν/ [τῇ σῇ] θεοσεβείᾳ καὶ προσαγορεύειν τὴν/ [ἀνε]φάμιλλόν σου καλοκἀγαθίαν/ [ἀδι]αλίπτως *κτλ*. Compare this with the καλοκ[ἀγαθίαν] of line 6 below (see note). The recipient is probably secular and of high rank.

If the original text of **301** did not extend very much beyond the preserved portion of the papyrus (see note to lines 12-13 below), then **301** would consist entirely of formulas and clichés. This suggests that **301** is little more than an acknowledgment sent to the recipient of earlier correspondence or of some favor or benefaction.

---

93 Other letters from the fourth century with some of these same elements include *P.Heid.* I 6 (Naldini, *Cristianesimo* no. 6) *P.Oxy.* XII 1494, and *P.Neph.* 4, 5, and 10. For a later example (dated 5th/6th century) and other parallels, see B. Mutschler, "Christlicher Brief an Mönche," *ZPE* 94 (1992), 105-114.

Recto: traces of letters ± 15 [
Ψεναμούνιος ἐπίσκ[(οπος)
ἐν κ(υρί)ῳ Θ(ε)ῷ χαίρει̣[ν.
σφόδρα ἐχάρην εὐκα̣ι̣[ρίαν εὑρὼν ἣν]
κατηξιώθην γράμματ̣[α πέμψαι]
π̣ρ̣ὸ̣ς τὴν ὑμῶν καλοκ[ἀγαθίαν καὶ]
ἅμα πάντα̣ς τοῦ εὐλογη̣[μένου ὑμῶν]
οἴκου μικροὺς καὶ μεγάλο[υς. οὐκ ἀν-]
απαύομαι νυκ̣[τὸ]ς καὶ ἡμ[έρας μνη-]
μ[ο]νεύω̣[ν] τὸ[ν] πόθον τ[ῆς ὑμετέρας]
ἀγάπης ἧ̣ς ἐ[δ]είξατε εἰ̣ς [
χ̣ι̣τω. ὁ̣ [Θ(εὸ)]ς̣ καὶ̣ ὁ Χ̣ρ(ιστὸ)ς αὐτ[οῦ φυλάξειαν]
ὑ̣μᾶ̣ς κα[ὶ . . .]σρ[.] . [

At left, vertical to text: τὴν ὑμῶν ἀδελφότητα

Verso: ἀπο[δός ?

2 papyrus επισκ/ 3 $\overline{κω}$ $\overline{Θω}$ 6 papyrus ϋμων 12 $\overline{χρς}$

(To) . . . (from) Psenamounios, bishop . . . greetings in the Lord God. I rejoice exceedingly having found the opportunity that I have been granted to send a letter to your Excellency together with all, great and small, of your blessed house. I do not cease to remember day and night the longing for the love which you have shown to . . . May God and his Christ preserve you and . . .

2 Ψεναμούνιος ἐπίσκ[There is a stroke across the bottom stroke of the kappa, presumably an abbreviation. If so, then something other than -πος could follow, but this appears unlikely. Something has to fill all the space of line 1, and it was customary for most titles, including ecclesiastical (except the less formal Αββα or Απα) to follow the name in

a letter, not precede it (Naldini, *Cristianesimo* nos. 21, 51, 95). It is more likely that the opening three lines are simply abbreviated and briefer than the body of the letter. This would be in keeping with the suggested character of the letter as little more than a brief acknowledgment. It is also possible that Ψεναμούνιος is a patronymic with the actual name of the bishop in the lost first line. If that were the case and if ἐπίσκ were an abbreviation for ἐπσκόπῳ, then the letter would have been addressed *to* the bishop, not *from* the bishop. However, the presence of καλοκἀγαθίαν in line 6 (see note below) makes this very unlikely.

4 σφόδρα ἐχάρην. The phrase is an epistolary convention; see Naldini, *Cristianesimo* page 201; Koskenniemi, *Studien* 75-77; *P.Mich.* VIII 482.23 (Naldini, *Cristianesimo* no. 1): ἐπὶ ἐχάρην λίαν λίαν/ ὡς σοῦ παραγενάμενος; *SB* XII 111253-4: ἐχάρην λίαν ἀκούσας ὅ[τι]/ ἐλύθης; *P.Petaus* 29.2-3: ἐχάρην πολλὰ ἀκούσασα ὅτε[ι] ἐσώθ[η]τε; *P.Yale* I 42.10-11: Πρωτολάου δὲ ἀπαγγείλαντος ἡμῖν τὰ κατὰ σέ, λίαν ἐχά[ρην]; *P.Yale* I 80.5-6: κἀγὼ ἐχάρην πόλλα ἀκούσας ὅτι ἥκι εἰς Τεπτυνιν; in the New Testament, 3 John 3. The use of σφόδρα instead of λίαν or πάνυ or πολλά seems a bit unusual. I found no instance of it in the Duke Data Bank of Documentary Papyri; but see *P.Oxy.* XIV 1676.4, ἐχάρην μεγάλως.

εὐκαι[ρίαν εὑρὼν ἦν] The best candidate for filling in the word are some form of εὐκαιρέω/εὐκαιρία, chiefly used to express motivation for one's own letter, Koskenniemi, *Studien* 77-87, especially 82, and Tibiletti, *Lettere* 80-82. ἐχάρην typically calls for an aorist participle; see the examples given in the preceding paragraph and compare *BGU* IV 1081.r2-3, εὐκαιρίαν εὑρὼν τοῦ πρὸς σὲ ἐρχομένου ἐχάρην *κτλ.* as well as *P.Abinn.* 30.r3-4, *P.Ant.* III 192.r3, *P.Fouad* 89.r1, *P.Oxy.* XVI 1861.r1-2.

5 κατηξιώθην. See Tibiletti, *Lettere* 71-2. There is an irreducible awkwardness here that is a result of combining so many conventions in two lines, particularly in the transition from εὐκαι[ρίαν εὑρών to κατηξιώθην, an unskillful conflation perhaps of epistolary clichés.

6 πρὸς τὴν. The rho is badly knocked out of place, and the eta is uncertain after close examination, but this remains the most probable reading.

καλοκἀγαθίαν. The word appears in the late fourth century in the papyrus record, but is not found much later. It is used in patristic literary letters exclusively for secular individuals, usually officials, Dinneen, *Titles* 38-9, 108 and Tibiletti, *Lettere* 37. See also *P.Amh.* II 145 (Naldini, *Cristianesimo* no. 49), a letter from a monk to someone evidently of influence, requesting a favor for a friend; H. Zilliacus, *Untersuchungen zu den abstrakten Anredeformen und Höflichkeitstiteln im Griechischen* (Helsinki 1949) 45.

6-8 πρὸς τὴν ὑμῶν καλοκ[ἀγαθίαν καὶ]/ ἅμα πάντας τοῦ εὐλογη[μένου σου]/ οἴκου. Compare *P.Genova* I 37.2-4 (fourth century): τὴν ὑμετέραν θεοφίλειαν καὶ εὔχο[μαι/ σωτηρίας καὶ ἅμα τοῦ εὐλογιμε[(undetermined text missing)/ μικροῦ and *PSI* VII 839.r3: εὐλογημένου σου οἴκου; *PSI* XIII 1345.14: τοῦ εὐλογημένου καὶ ἀφθόνου ὑμῶν οἴκου.

7-8 ἅμα πάντας τοῦ εὐλογη[μένου ὑμῶν]/ οἴκου μικροὺς καὶ μεγάλο[υς. Compare *P.Lips.* 111.18-19 (fourth century): 'Ασπάζ[ομ]έν σε πάντες οἱ ἐν τ[ῇ]/ οἰκίᾳ μικρούς τε καὶ μεγάλους; *P.Neph.* 12.16-17 (fourth century): ἀσπάζομαι τοὺς ἐν τῇ μοναστηρίῳ πᾶσι, μικροὺς καὶ μεγάλους; *P.Haun.* III 58.r5-7 (AD 439): (eleven names) πρεσβυτέροις καὶ (five names) διακόνοις καὶ λοιποῖς μικροῖς καὶ μεγάλοις τῶν ἀπὸ κώμης Καρανίδος; *P.Oxy.* LIX 4005.r9-10 (sixth century): πολλὰ δὲ προσαγορεύομεν ἀπὸ μικροῦ ἕως μεγάλους τὴν σὴν διάθεσιν. The phrase μικροὺς καὶ μεγάλους also appears in the very fragmentary *P.Ness.* III 165.7-8. *P.Genova* I 37.3-4 (sixth-seventh century) has the phrase καὶ ἅμα τοῦ εὐλογιμε [(undetermined text missing)/ μικροῦ. *P.Lips.* 111 is evidently secular, though its author may be Christian; the rest are all monastic or ecclesiastical.

8-10 οὐκ ἀναπαύομαι *κτλ.* The whole phrase has a history stretching over many centuries. Compare *P.Giss.* 19.7-9 (second century BC): [ἀλλὰ συν]εχῶς ἀγρυπνοῦσα νυκτὸς ἡ-/[μέρας μ]ίαν μέριμναν ἔχω τὴν περὶ/ [τῆς σωτ]ηρίας σου, and, much closer in style to **301**, *P.Grenf.* II 91.5 (sixth/ seventh century) to ἀββᾷ Πέτρῳ ἐπισκ(όπῳ): καὶ οὐ παυόμεθα εὐχόμενοι νύκτα καὶ ἡμέραν ὑπὲρ τῆς σωτηρίας ὑμῶν. See Koskenniemi, *Studien* 128-30.

νυκτὸς καὶ ἡμέρας. Compare also *P.Lond.* III 1244 p. 244 (Naldini, *Cristianesimo* no. 58).2: Προηκουμένως πολλά σε προσαγορεύω νυκτὸς καὶ ἡμέραις τῷ ὑψίστῳ θεῷ; *Museum Helveticum* 18 (1961) 24-27 lines 4-5 (Naldini, *Cristianesimo* no. 53). Also compare Basil, *Epistulae* 226: Αὐτοῦ οὖν τούτου ἕνεκεν ἀπεστείλαμεν . . . Μελέτιον . . . ὃς διηγήσεται ὑμῖν τὸν ἡμέτερον πόθον ὃν ἔχομεν ἐφ' ὑμῖν, καὶ τὴν μέριμναν τῶν ψυχῶν ἡμῶν, ὅτι νυκτὸς καὶ ἡμέρας δεόμεθα τοῦ Κυρίου περὶ τῆς ὑμῶν εὐδοκιμήσεως *κτλ.*; *Epistulae* 267: διὰ τοῦ γράμματος ἀναπαύω τὸν πόθον ὃν ἔχω ἐπὶ τῇ ἀπολαύσει τῶν ἐν σοὶ καλῶν *κτλ.*; Gregory of Nazianzus *Epistulae* 42.1: ὥστε με δυνηθῆναι διαβῆναι πρὸς τὴν ὑμετέραν ἀγάπην καὶ τόν τε πόθον, ὃν ἔχω ἐφ' ὑμῖν, ἀναπαῦσαι *κτλ*.

10-11 τὸ[ν] πόθον τ[ῆς ὑμετέρας]/ ἀγάπης ἧς ἐ[δ]είξατε. Compare Basil, *Epistulae* 140.1: καταπαύσω τὸν πόθον ὃν ἔχω ἐπὶ τῇ συντυχίᾳ τῆς ὑμετέρας ἀγάπης. John Chrysostom, *In principium Actorum* 1.29-30, (PG51.87), ὅταν ἴδῃ τὸν πόθον τῆς ὑμετέρας ἀγάπης, *κτλ*.

12 χ̣ι̣τω The reading is difficult, and I can find no satisfactory way to fill the lacuna from the preceding line.

ὁ̣ [Θ(εὸ)]ς καὶ ὁ Χρ(ιστὸ)ς αὐτ[οῦ. Compare *P.Lond.* VI 1929.3: ὁ π[α]ντοκ[ράτωρ] θεὸς καὶ ὁ Χρι[στὸς] αὐτοῦ.

ὁ̣ [Θ(εὸ)]ς καὶ ὁ Χ̣ρ(ιστὸ)ς αὐτ[οῦ φυλάξειαν]/ ὑ̣μᾶ̣ς This seems the most probable restoration, given the likely amount of space and the plural subject. Some aorist optative or subjunctive form of φυλάττω or (more commonly) διαφυλάττω in this position is a Christian cliché; see Tibiletti, *Lettere* 64-66. It typically occurs in closing formulas, which raises the possibility that with lines 12 and 13 we are near the end of **301** and have lost little of the bottom text. Compare *P.Abinn.* 6.25-6: ὁ κύριος ὁ θεὸς διαφυλάξι σε, as well as *P.Abinn.* 8.28-9, *P.Cair.Masp.* I 67005.r27, *P.Herm.* 8.22-3, *P.Lond.* VI 1923.22-23, *SB* VI 9107.r3, *P.Neph.* 1.31, to give only a few examples. For more discussion and bibliography, see the editor's note for *P.Berl.Sarischouli* 17.r4 (seventh century): ὁ κύριος ἐν ὑγιείᾳ ὑμᾶς διαφυλάξοι.

Line at the side. ἀδελφότητα. The word in the New Testament refers to the Christian community (1 Peter 2:17, 5:9); was used occasionally by the early Fathers and frequently in the fourth century, with different shades of meaning; and was applied to religious communities by the Cappadocians, Palladius, and Macarius (PGL s.v.), e.g., Gregory of Nazianzus, letter 238 to a community of monks and nuns: Τῇ εὐλαβεστάτῃ καὶ πάντα κεκοσμημένῃ ἐν Χριστῷ ἀδελφότητι (Gallay edition, 2:128). It is not found in papyri before the fourth century (Zilliacus, 47), where it is a form of address; see *P.Lond.* VI 1915.11, πρὸς τὴν ἀδελφότητα ὑμῶν; *P.Herm.* 45.1-3, where the reference is ambiguous; and *P.Stras.* I 35.16 (Naldini, *Cristianesimo* no. 96), ἡ σὴ ἀδελφότης. Naldini, *Cristianesimo* 368 suggests that this last is a "religious superior," but see the objections of Ewa Wipszycka, "Remarques sur les lettres privées chrétiennes des IIe - IVe siècles," *JJurPap* 18 (1974) 202. If the καλοκἀγαθίαν of line 6 does indeed indicate a secular official, it would appear to support Wipszycka.

302. Letter Concerning a Bishop

Inv. 167 | 32 x 17.2 cm. | VI

Pl. 10 | | Provenance unknown

The text is a letter of which both the author and the recipient are unknown. As commonly in sixth century papyri, there is no introductory greeting, and the few traces of ink on the verso, probably the address, are no longer legible. Some ink extends down from the top edge. This probably belongs to a different document; the distance between the top edge and the first line is greater than that between any two lines of text. The ink is faded in places and holes make reading difficult in the fourth line, but the text is clear for much the greater part. The papyrus is broken in two by a vertical fold in the middle.

The hand is very cursive, with letters now large and written with a flourish, now small and cramped, making it difficult to compare with more regular documentary hands. It is probably sixth century (compare with the plates in *P.Cair.Masp.* I-III especially no. 67032, plates 22-3, and no. 67030, plate 20), but possibly earlier (compare *P.Oxy.* XVI 1878, plate 1, dated 461 AD).

The author of the letter says nothing directly about himself. However, in his closing salutation, he mentions οἱ καθοσιωμένοι ἄνδρες, "the dedicated men." Although used in the sixth century as a polite epithet (e.g., *P.Oxy.* XVI 1855.1 and 4; 1868.4; 1966.3), the principal use of the term καθοσιωμένοι was military.[94] The phrase here could refer to a company of soldiers.

The recipient is addressed as ἡ σὴ μεγαλοπρέπια and τὸ σὸν μέγεθος. By the sixth century, μεγαλοπρέπια and related forms were used to address a range of functionaries, from local officials to the *praeses* or

---

[94] O. Hornickel, *Ehren- und Rangprädikate in den Papyruskunden* (Giessen 1930) 18.

higher.[95] Μέγεθος is less common. In one case it is used for a στρατηλάτης (*P.Lond.* V 1786.2, 30—fifth century); in another, a κόμης (*P.Oxy.* I 155.7, 8, 9). It is used in a formula in legal petitions of the sixth century for the *praeses* (*P.Oxy.* XVI 1876.3; 1877.3; 1878.3). Both terms are used for secular officials and laymen of high rank in patristic letters.[96]

The letter concerns a bishop. We cannot know what he was bishop *of*. It may have been Alexandria, as line 1 suggests, but this is far from certain. He is not referred to by any appropriate title such as patriarch, archbishop, or even Παπας. He could as easily have been a bishop from the Thebaid (line 4). The letter would be from someone sent after him who failed to catch up.

The letter is presumably about some interaction between the higher civil and ecclesiastical authorities. There were certainly some overlapping jurisdictions and shared responsibilities between the two by the sixth century. Theoretically at least, considerable civil power was granted to bishops by imperial legislation.[97] Bishops could, for example, adjudicate law suits, but only if both parties agreed to accept the verdict. Clergy and monks could be tried by ecclesiastical courts, though this was a defined and limited privilege. Under Anastasius, bishops in the east, with other local worthies, could take part in the election of local authorities such as the σιτώνης or *defensor civitatis*, and they participated in the *concilium provinciae*.[98] Bishops also controlled extensive properties and so had an important public role, including obligations as revenue collectors for the state.[99]

---

95 G. Rouillard, *L'Administration civile de l'Égypte byzantine*, 2nd ed. (Paris 1928) 48, 54; Hornickel 28-9.

96 Dinneen, *Titles* 40, 45, 108.

97 See the references in B. Biondi, *Il diritto romano cristiano* (Milan 1952) 1: 435-61.

98 *Codex Justinianus* 1.4.7-8; 1.4.29; 1.4.17, 19; see Jones, *Later Roman Empire* 480, 491-2, 758-9, 763-6.

99 J. Gascou, "Les grands domaines, la cité et l'état en Égypte byzantine," *T&MByz* 9 (1983) 1-89 (see the summary on 60); Wipszycka, *Ressources* 34-56.

A. Steinwenter, "Die Stellung der Bischöfe in der Byzantischen Verwaltung Ägyptens," *Studi in onore di Pietro de Francisci* (Milan 1956) 1: 75-99, has tried to show that the documentary evidence of episcopal activity in Egypt gives little support to any exercise of the authority given to bishops by imperial legislation, at least outside of the *episcopalis audientia*. His argument, however, is based largely on silence. For a more positive estimate of episcopal civil authority, see Jean Durliat, "Les attributions civiles des Éveques byzantins: l'exemple du diocèse d'Afrique (533-709)" *JŒByz* 32 (1982) 73-83.

The patriarchs of Alexandria exercised secular authority in varying degrees over the years. Paul the Tabennesiot (537-539) was given extraordinary power by Justinian to appoint and remove civil and military officers. Eulogius (581-608) effectively took charge of the government amidst the anarchy of a revolt. Cyrus, the last patriarch before the Arab conquest, was both pope and prefect.[100]

While it is impossible to be certain what the letter is all about, two possibilities suggest themselves. The first concerns the military *annona.* By the sixth century, troops received their requisitions directly from the region in which they were stationed.[101] A law of the emperor Anastasius (491-505) declared that bishops were to have a part in handling the military *annona,* together with the governor *(praeses)* and *defensor,* presumably to keep the process fair:

> Οἱ ὑφεστῶτες καὶ τῇ παραφυλακῇ προσκαρτεροῦντες στρατιῶται ἐν τοῖς σεδέτοις αὐτῶν τὸ προσφερόμενον εἶδος ἐκ τῶν ἐν τῇ πόλει ἢ τῇ ἐνορίᾳ αὐτῆς γεωργουμένων δεχέσθωσαν ὑπὲρ τῶν ἀννόνων αὐτῶν δοκιμασίᾳ τοῦ ἐπισκόπου καὶ τοῦ ἄρχοντος ἢ τοῦ ἐκδίκου ἐξ ἀπολείψεως τοῦ ἄρχοντος, καὶ οὔκ ἀναγκάζεται ὁ συντελεστὴς ἀπαργυρισμὸν διδόναι. (*Codex Justinianus* I.4.18)[102]

> Those soldiers stationed and remaining at the garrison shall receive payment-in-kind in their cantonments from produce in the city or its territory for their annona after inspection by the bishop and the archon or ekdikos in the absence of the archon, and the collector shall not be forced to give cash-for-value.

If an official were unable to proceed with distributing needed supplies without the bishop, this would explain why someone was sent after him, and why a company of καθοσιωμένοι ἄνδρες would be so grateful.[103]

---

[100] Liberatus, *Breviarium* 23 (PL 68.1045); Jean Maspero, *Histoire des Patriarches d'Alexandrie depuis la mort de l'empereur Anastase jusqu'à la réconciliation des églises jacobites (518-616)* (Paris 1923) 139, 268.

[101] A. Johnson and L. West, *Byzantine Egypt: Economic Studies* (Princeton 1949) 215-229.

[102] See LSJ s.v. for the correct reading of σέδετον.

[103] The church was also employed by the state in the handling and transportation of the *annona civica;* see R. Remondon, "Le monastère Alexandrin de la Métanoia," *Studi di onore di Edoardo Volterra,* Bd. 5 (Milan 1971) 769-781.

The second possibility concerns civic affairs. Justinian charged the local bishop, together with five other leading citizens, with appointing administrators to handle civic funds, checking the books once a year, and removing any administrator on evidence of dishonesty:

> . . . ἀλλὰ τὸν ἑκάστης πόλεως ὁσιώτατον ἐπίσκοπον καὶ τοὺς πρωτεύοντας τῆς πόλεως, οὐ μὴν ἀλλὰ καὶ τοὺς αὐτῆς κτήτορας προβάλλεσθαι μὲν τὸν πατέρα τὸν τῆς πόλεως καὶ τὸν σιτώνην καὶ ἄλλους τοιούτους διοικητάς . . . εἴ τις δὲ ἐκ τῶν εἰρημένων διοικητῶν ἀνεπιτήδειος εὑρεθείη, παραχρῆμα τοῦτον ἀποκινεῖσθαι κελεύομεν καὶ ἄλλον ἀντ' αὐτοῦ ὑπό τε τοῦ ὁσιωτάτου τῆς πόλεως ἐπισκόπου ὑπό τε τῶν λοιπῶν κτητόρων, καθὼς εἴρηται, προβάλλεσθαι. (*Novellae* 128.16)[104]

> But (we command) that the most holy bishop of each city and the leading citizens of the city, not only but including its property owners, choose the City Father and the sitones and such other treasurers . . . if any of the aforementioned treasurers should be found unfit, we command that he be removed immediately, and another be selected in his place by the most holy bishop of the city and the remaining property owners, as set out above.

302 says that the recipient, "knowing the force of the πρόσταγμα," should remind the bishop together "with the others." Could the others be the πρωτεύοντες τῆς πόλεως?[105]

1 καταλαβὼν τὴν Ἀλεξανδρέων ἔγνων τὸν εὐλαβ(έστατον) ἐπίσκοπον ἀποπλεῦσαι
ἐπὶ τὸ Πηλούσιον· συνήθως τύνυν εὐδοκιμοῦσα ἡ σὴ μεγαλοπρέ(πεια) εἰδυῖα
τὴν δύναμιν τοῦ προστάγματος κελεύσῃ τοῦτον ὑπομνησθῆναι μετὰ τῶν
4 ἄλλων πρὸς τὼ ̣ ̣ ̣ ̣ ρε ̣α ̣τομε ̣ἀ̣π̣ὸ̣ Θηβαίδο̣ς εὑρ[ε]ῖν τὸ πρᾶγμα

---

104 Cf. *Codex Justinianus* 1.4.26, where the bishop is similarly ordered to oversee public construction with three other leading citizens.

105 Cf. *P.Mich.* XVIII 795, a V/VI century memorandum (ὑπομνηστικόν—cf. line 3, ὑπομνησθῆναι) for an order to certain *curiales* of Pelusium regarding the fair distribution of olive oil, with a decision to be made "in the presence of all those who have been ordered," παρόντων πάντων τῶν προστεταγμένω̣ν—cf. line 3, τὴν δύναμιν τοῦ προστάγματος.

ἕτυμον, εἵνα κἀγὼ συνήθως εὐχαριστήσω τῇ σῇ
μεγαλοπρέπιᾳ
καὶ οἱ καθοσιωμένοι ἄνδρες συνήθως καὶ αὐτοὶ κηρύξωσιν
[τ]ὸ σὸν
μέγεθος.

1 εὐλαβ' = εὐλαβέστατον 2, 5 μεγαλοπρ`ε´, μεγαλοπρεπία = μεγαλοπρεπεία 2 τύνυν = τοίνυν 4 πρὸς τὼ = πρὸς τὸ
5 ἕτυμον = ἕτοιμον εἵνα = ἵνα

Arriving in the city of the Alexandrians, I learned that the most pious bishop had sailed away to Pelusium; therefore, will your Magnificence, with your customary grace (?), knowing the force of the decree, order that he be reminded with the others . . . . . from the Thebaid to find the matter ready, so that I too as usual may thank your magnificence and so that the dedicated men, as usual, may also themselves proclaim your greatness.

1 εὐλαβ(έστατον). Εὐλαβεία and εὐλαβέστατος are common in sixth century letters; see the index of *P.Oxy.* XVI. The terms are applied to both secular and ecclesiastical individuals; compare *P.Oxy.* XVI 1839.6, 1856.3, 5, 187510 (secular) with 1847.1, 1871.7, 1890.8, 1900.6 (ecclesiastical; see also *P.Flor.* I 73.3, 7). Dinneen, *Titles* 23-25 translated it as "most pious" and found it common for clergy, unusual for laity in patristic letters. The editors of *P.Oxy.* XVI chose to translate all but one of the above cited cases as "discretion," "discreet," or "most discreet," including a "most discreet monk." In the case of clergy, a better translation is surely "pious" and "reverend," as the translator of *P.Oxy.* XVI 1871 realized.

2 Τοίνυν is usually postpositive, though not always so in later periods (LSJ s.v.), so it seems best to put the break between Πηλούσιον and συνήθως rather than συνηθῶς and τοίνυν. Also, συνήθως makes more sense with the following participle; cf. *P.Oxy.* XVI 1864.8-9 and 1872.2: καταξιώσῃ ⟨ἡ σὴ⟩ διάθεσις συνήθος καταξιοῦσα φιλῖν συνκροτῆσε τὸν/ εὐγε[ν]ῆ Παῦλον *κτλ.*

Εὐδόκιμος is common in Byzantine papyri, any forms of εὐδοκιμέω much less so. I have found only one so far, σε εὐδοκιμοῦντα in

P.Oxy. XVI 1870.4-5, translated as "your pleasing state." Here with συνηθῶς it probably means "pleasing as usual," "in your customary pleasing manner" or "with your customary grace." Compare with the two uses of συνήθως plus participle mentioned above.

5 Πρόσταγμα. The term was widely used and broadly applied by the Byzantine period, but appears to have been employed mainly by provincial governors and higher, particularly for tax matters. When used by the *praeses Thebaidis,* it usually refers to the *annona*—see Józef Modrzejewski, "The *prostagma* in the papyri," *JJurPap* 5 (1951) 203-5.

303. Order for Payment

Inv. 416 | 15.2 x 5.6 cm. | 2 September 515
Pl. 11 | | Oxyrhynchus

The papyrus is badly damaged. A fold in the center has made it nearly impossible to read much of the text in the second line, which unhappily is where we should most like to be able to read it. The second hand in line three is a cursive so rapid and stylized that it is nearly illegible; the reading can be supplied only by reference to the formula.

The document is an order for oil to be delivered to a monastery. There is little that is unique or unusual about it. Such orders for deliveries are common in sixth century papyri and closely follow a formula, e.g., the small archive of such documents in *SB* XIV 12124-12126 and *BGU* III 960-966, orders for oil deliveries from one Theon to the oil manufacturer Sambas.[106] Similar payments or gifts to monks or monasteries from this period are *P.Rain.Cent.* 133, *P.Oxy.* VI 994, and *P.Oxy.* XVI 1945.

The only serious question about the document is the interpretation of ἐποικίου or ἐποίκιον in line 2, something which might be clearer if the text following it were better preserved. The best reading is εποικ with a stroke across the bottom of the kappa, abbreviating ἐποίκιον. We should expect the name of the village to follow and perhaps some mention of the purpose of the gift or payment, or possibly some other means of identifying the particular monastery, but it is impossible to be certain (see the note on line 2 below).

ἐποίκιον has been variously translated as "village," "hamlet," or "farmstead." The confusion arises in part from the growth and

106 On this archive, see F. Mitthof, "Das Archiv des elaiourgos Sambas," *ZPE* 103 (1994) 53-84.

development of some ἐποίκια into full κῶμαι, villages.[107] In its origin, however, an ἐποίκιον "was basically a building complex which functioned as the centre of an agricultural property" and which had no independent administration.[108]

I can find no instance in which a monastery was simply identified with an ἐποίκιον, although that does not mean it was impossible. By the sixth century many monasteries were quite substantial, but it does not follow that all were so large that nothing referred to as a monastery could be located within an ἐποίκιον. *P.Rain.Cent.* 133, dated fifth or sixth century, is a brief order for wood to be delivered to τὸ ἐποίκιον Αἰλιανοῦ/ εἰς οἰκοδομὴν τοῦ μοναστηρίου, but this only demonstrates proximity.

Is this monastery perhaps the owner of the ἐποίκιον? Monasteries were not substantial land owners in the fourth century.[109] However, they controlled large estates by the sixth.

† Μακρόβ̣ι̣ο̣ς λαμπρό(τατος) *vacat*
παράσχου εἰς τὸ μοναστ̣ή̣ρ̣ιο̣ν̣ ἐπ̣ο̣[ι]κ(ίου) ε̣ἰ̣ς̣
κ̣αταλ̣[̣ ̣] ̣[̣] ̣ ̣[̣ ἐ]λ̣α̣ί̣[ου] ξ̣έ̣σ̣τ̣α̣ς̣
πέν̣τ̣ε, γί(νονται) ἐλαί(ου) ξ(έσται) ε μ(όνοι)
(2nd h.) † σεσημίω(μαι) ἐλ(αίου) ξ(έστας) πέντε μόν(ους)
4 (1st h.) (ἔτους)] ρ̣ϙβ ρξα Θωθ ε ἀρχ(ῆ̣) θ ἰνδ(ικτίονος) *vacat*

1 papyrus λαμπρ`ο'/ 2 papyrus εποικ/
3 σεσημίω(μαι) = σεσημείωμαι 4 papyrus ινδ`ο'/

---

107 See M. Drew-Bear, *Le Nome Hermopolite: Toponymes et sites* (Missoula 1979) 41-42.

108 D. Rathbone, *Economic Rationalism and Rural Society in Third-Century A.D. Egypt* (Cambridge 1991) 31-32. He includes a reconstruction of the ἐποίκιον described in *P.Mich.* XI 620.

109 E. Wipszycka, "Les terres de la congrégation pachômienne dans une liste de payements pour les apora," in *Le monde grec. Hommages à Cl. Préaux* (Brussels 1975), claimed that a tax register of 367/8 showed a monastery which owned an ἐποίκιον; see however Bagnall, *Egypt* 290 and note 169.

(1st hand) (From) Makrobios most splendid. Supply to the monastery of the village . . . five pints of oil, total five pints of oil only. (2nd h.) I have noted (*or* authorized) five pints of oil only. (1st h.) Year 192 and 161, Thoth 5 at the beginning of the 9th indiction.

1 Μακρόβιος λαμπρότατος. This may very well be the same Makrobios, also λαμπρότατος, of *P.Oxy.* XVI 2003. The title λαμπρότατος was exclusively for laymen of high rank, Dinneen, *Titles* 39, 108, Tibiletti, *Lettere* 36. By the sixth century, λαμπρότατος was used so broadly that the rank or office of the holder cannot be identified by the title alone; see A. Arjava, "Zum Gebrauch der griechischen Rangprädikate des Senatorenstandes in den Papyri und Inschriften," *Tyche* 6 (1991) 18-24.

1, 4 λαμπρό(τατος), ινδ(ικτίονος). The omicron before the abbreviating stroke is a small letter written just above the line and over the stroke in both cases.

2 παράσχου εἰς τὸ. It is far more common in such documents for παράσχου to be followed by the actual recipients, who are named in the dative, rather than the location, but there is nothing against such a locution. Εἰς is the all-purpose preposition for such documents; in *P.Rain.Cent.* 133 it is used three times in three lines, each time in a different sense (the German translation uses *in, zu,* and *für*).

εἰς καταλ[. While the καταλ is fairly clear, the reading of εἰς after ἐποικ(ίου) is very uncertain, so uncertain that πε is also possible. However, I can find no village or hamlet with a name that begins Πεκατα in P. Pruneti, *I centri abitati dell'Ossirinchite: repertorio toponomastico* (Firenze 1981) or in the Duke Data Bank. If the reading of εἰς is correct, then the text might be restored as εἰς κατάλεπτα, "for minor expenses," or better εἰς καταλείφειν, "for anointing"; cf. *P.Oxy.* XVI 1945, in which wine is provided to some monks εἰς π(ε)ῖν.

3 μόν(ους). By the end of the third line, the hand has become so cursive that almost any reading could be justified. However, the formula is so invariable that either this or μόν(ον) is almost certainly the correct reading.

BIBLIOGRAPHY

The following volumes are cited by short title or abbreviation:

LSJ = *A Greek-English Lexicon: with a Supplement,* ed. H. G. Liddell and R. Scott, rev. and aug. H. S. Jones, 9th ed., with Revised Supplement by P. G. Glare (Oxford 1940, 1968, 1996)

PG = *Patrologia cursus completus: Series graeca,* ed. Jacques-Paul Migne (Paris 1857-1887)

PL = *Patrologia cursus completus: Series latina,* ed. Jacques-Paul Migne (Paris 1864-1884)

PGL = *A Patristic Greek Lexicon,* ed. G. W. H. Lampe (Oxford 1961)

New Docs = *New Documents Illustrating Early Christianity* ed. G.H.R. Horsley (North Ryde, NSW : The Ancient History Documentary Research Centre, Macquarie University 1983-94), volumes 1- 7

Bagnall, *Egypt* = Roger Bagnall, *Egypt in Late Antiquity* (Princeton 1993)

Chitty, *Desert* = Derwas Chitty, *The Desert a City : an introduction to the study of Egyptian and Palestinian monasticism under the Christian Empire* (Oxford 1966)

Daniélou, *Bible and Liturgy* = Jean Daniélou, *The Bible and the Liturgy,* (Notre Dame 1956)

Dinneen, *Titles* = Sister Lucilla Dinneen, *Titles of Address in Christian Greek Epistolography to 527 A. D.* (Washington 1929)

Gignac, *Grammar* = F.T. Gignac, *A Grammar of the Greek Papyri of the Roman and Byzantine Periods* (Milan 1981)

Jones, *Later Roman Empire* = A. H. M. Jones, *The Later Roman Empire, 284-602; a social, economic and administrative survey* (Oxford 1964)

Kim, *Familiar Letter* = Chan-Hie Kim, *Form and Structure of the Familiar Greek Letter of Recommendation,* Dissertation Series, no. 4 (Missoula 1972)

Koskenniemi, *Studien* = H. Koskenniemi, *Studien zur Idee nd Phraseologie des griechischen Briefes bis 400 n. Chr.* (Helsinki 1956)

Montevecchi, *La Papirologia* = O. Montevecchi, *La Papirologia* 2nd ed. (Turin 1988)

Naldini, *Cristianesimo* = Mario Naldini, *Il Cristianesimo in Egitto: Lettere private nei papiri dei secoli II- IV,* Studi e testi di papirologia, no. 3 (Firenze 1968)

Paap, *Nomina Sacra* = A. H. R. E. Paap, *The Nomina Sacra of the First Five Centuries,* Papyrologica Lugduno-Batava 8 (Leiden 1959)

Preisigke, *Wörterbuch* = F. Preisigke, *Wörterbuch der griechische Papyrusurkunden* (Berlin 1925)

Roberts, *Manuscript* = C. H. Roberts, *Manuscript, Society and Belief in Early Christian Egypt* (London 1979)

Seider, *Paläographie* = Richard Seider, *Paläographie der griechischen Papyri* (Stuttgart 1967-70)

Tibiletti, *Lettere* = Giuseppe Tibiletti, *Le lettere private nei papiri greci del III e IV secolo d.C.: Tra paganesimo e cristianesimo,* Scienze filologiche e letteratura 15 (Milan 1979)

van Haelst, *Catalogue* = J. van Haelst, *Catalogue des Papyrus littéraires juifs et chrétiens* (Sorbonne Serie "Papyrologie" 1, Paris 1976)

White, *Ancient Letters* = John L. White, *Light From Ancient Letters* (Philadelphia 1986)

Wipszycka, *Ressources* = Ewa Wipszycka, *Les ressources et les activités économiques des églises en Égypte du IVe au VIIIe siècle* (Pap. Brux. 10, Brussels 1972)

Indices

Square brackets [ ] indicate that the word has been either wholly or substantially supplied, either by conjecture or from other sources.

Part 1: Literary/Liturgical Texts

No. 293 (Matt. 6: 4-6, 8-12) and 294 recto (Ps. 150 3b-6)

No. 294 verso and Nos. 295 and 296

Part 2: Documentary Texts

I Chronology

A. Oxyrhynchite era

B. Months, days

C. Indictions

II Personal Names

III Geographical

IV Religion

V Official terms and titles

VI Professions, trades, occupations

VII Measures

VIII General Index

Concordance

Numbers: Inventory - Publication - Dissertation

Inventory	*Publication*	*Dissertation*
97	294	2
126	301	9
148	298	6
167	302	10
174b	299	7
416	303	
417	300	8
455b	295	3
466a	297	5
488	296	4
571	293	1

METRIC 1 2 3 4 5 6 7 8 9
Col Inv 571
12 11 10 9

METRIC 1 2 3 4 5 6 7 8
Col Inv 571
12 11 10 9

INV. 455b

P. Col. Inv. 488

P. Col. 466A

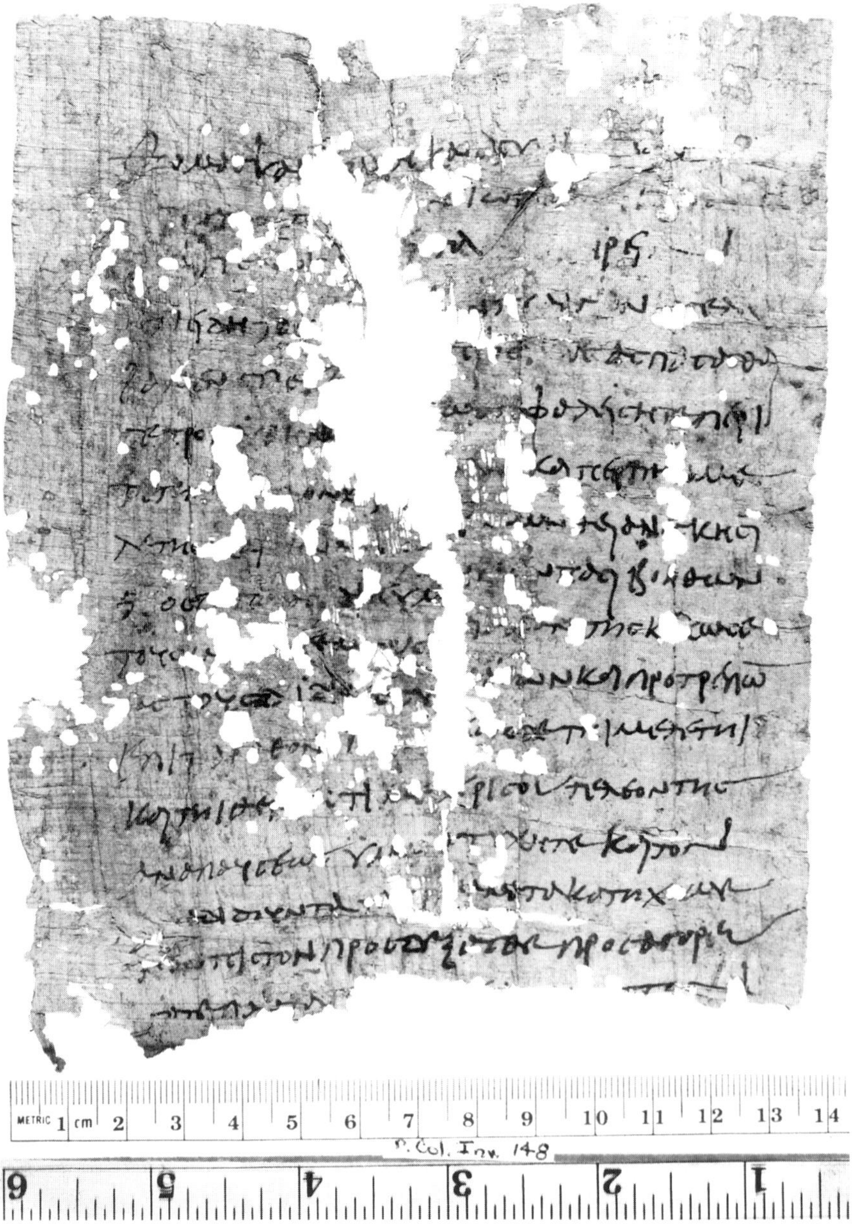
P. Col. Inv. 148

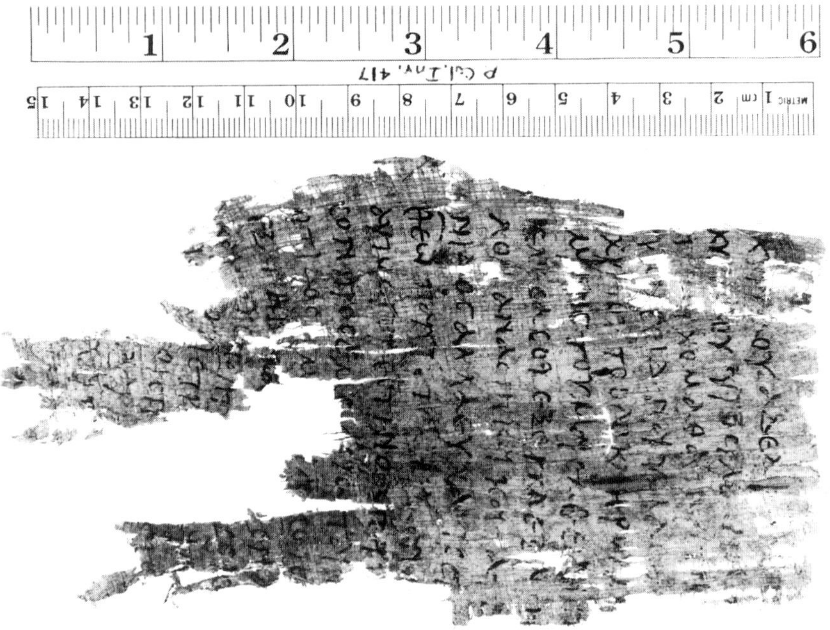

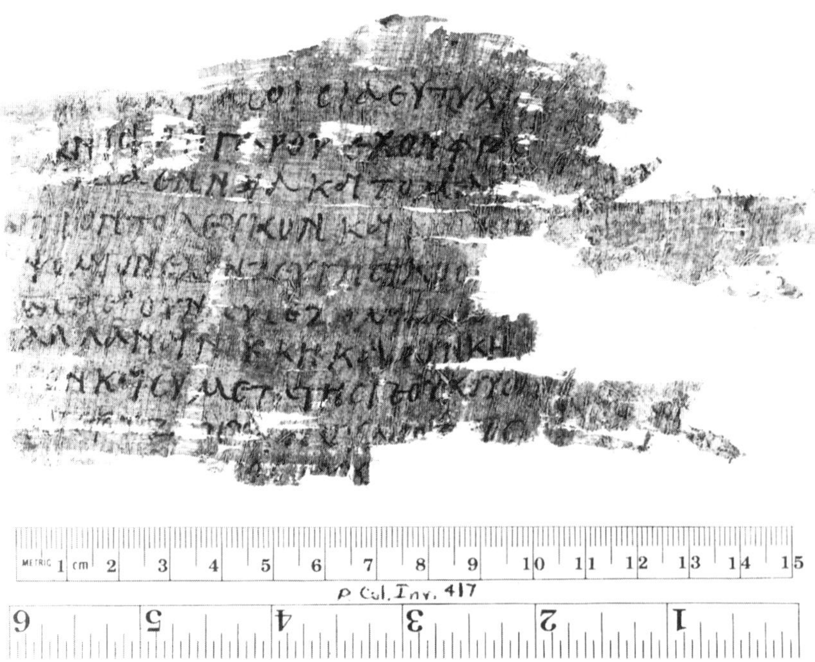
P Col. Inv. 417

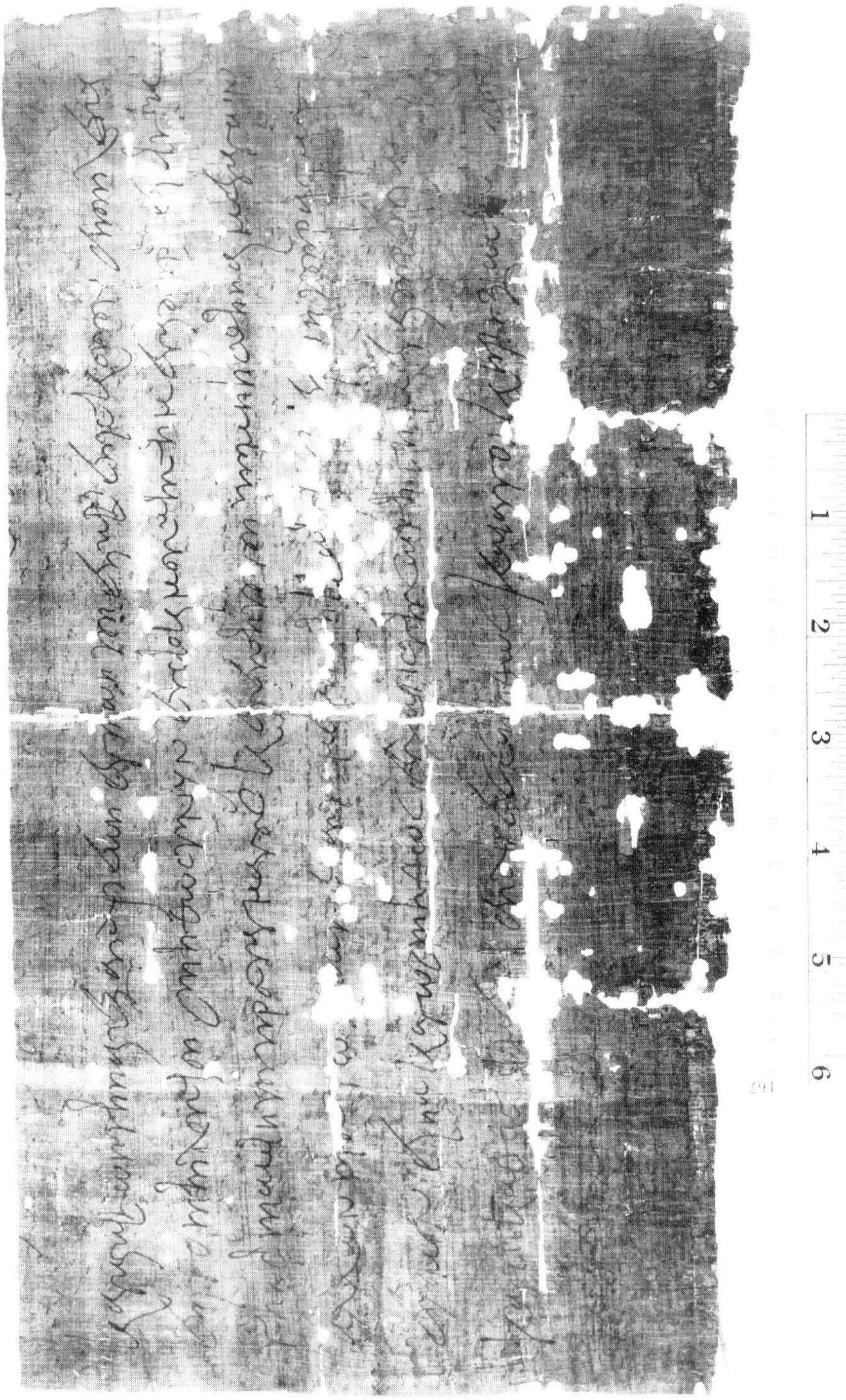